AF378215

FOOD
TRUCK
FEASTS

WORLD RECIPES FROM
THE STREET TO YOUR KITCHEN

FOOD TRUCK FEASTS

ERIKA BUDIMAN

hardie grant publishing

CONTENTS

citi
BANH MI BOYS
VIETNAMESE STREET FOOD
FareShare
Tel 9428 0044
www.fareshare.net.au
rescuing food, fighting hunger
LetsDo

INTRODUCTION

Roy Choi, owner of the LA-based food business Kogi, is the unofficial godfather or pioneer of the modern food truck. Far beyond the mobile lunch cantinas at construction sites, Roy began serving bold, restaurant-quality Korean and Mexican food at street-food prices from a truck in 2008. Since then the phenomenon has spread internationally.

But who would have thought that Australia could forge its own food truck culture and community within the space of just a few years? Australia is a rich and thriving multicultural nation for which food is the ultimate celebration of its diversity. In the fast-changing, ever-reinventing culinary landscapes of cities like Melbourne and Sydney, some may briefly lament the closing of one food outlet, but eagerly anticipate the opening of another. So it is not surprising that Australians have embraced this new mode of eating with eager arms. A new breed of food trucks first appeared in Australia as early as 2010. Since then the scene has quickly gained momentum, with new trucks being announced through social media at an almost alarming rate.

Sure, Australians have seen food trucks before – the most popular one being the pastel-coloured Mr Whippy ice-cream vans – but not with the kind of quality dishes that we get to enjoy now. And according to Bill Jacobs, owner and operator of Dos Diablos Mobile Cantina (see p. 150), 'Australia is quite an irreverent, informal culture, so the idea of being able to grab a six pack [of beers] or bottle of wine, head down to the park or beach and enjoy some quality food with friends just seems such an ideal fit.'

Like Bill, food trucks just make sense to me. I love the idea of being able to rustle up a group of friends with picnic blankets, some drinks, ball games and children in tow, and be able to head out to a local park or garden, and not have to worry about bringing your own food. Where else could you go at a moment's notice, with a large group of people including kids, and get restaurant-quality foods that will cater for the fussiest of tastes and appetites, all without having to wait for a table or make a reservation?

Yarraville Gardens, an inner-city park in Melbourne, has become a regular mini truck jam, thanks to a liberal local council. Most Wednesdays to Sundays, a small carnival of trucks bring you larger-than-life 'picnic feasts', showcasing food from all around the world. You may find foods such as wood-fired pizza, tacos, rice-noodle salads, pho soups, mushroom burgers, curries, Cajun gumbos, maybe even crocodile burgers. With such a smorgasboard your entrées and mains are definitely covered. And if you're still hungry, there's a choice of crème brûlée, 'fro-yo' or Spanish churros for dessert.

Australia's food truck community is generally easy-going, supportive and welcoming. It's not uncommon for resources and experiences to be shared. Between truck amigos, it's also a given to feed each other at the end of a busy night, or perhaps play ball games and pranks on one another during a quiet spell. I know of no other hospitality industry that can boast this kind of camaraderie.

Having said this, Australian food truck owners face many challenges. Local councils are generally responsible for handing out street permits, but with no precedence set, they are slow to support this new mode of dining, often under pressure from bricks-and-mortar businesses feeling threatened by this seeming competition. The number of street trading spots also hasn't kept up with the growth of the industry, so trucks often find themselves jostling for space. Added to this are extreme weather conditions and the fact that as a sole trader, you are responsible for everything. You're the buyer, the cook, the cleaner, the mechanic, the marketing department and bookkeeper.

And yet the attraction of setting up a food truck is still strong enough to encourage many young, brazen entrepreneurs – many with limited hospitality experience – to try their hand in a mobile food venture. Other owners have years of hospitality experience behind them and are attracted to the idea of being their own boss and being closer to their customers. Jim White from Smokin' Barrys (see p. 026) knows too well that, 'It shows very quickly how passionate you are or aren't [about your business] because there is nowhere to hide when you are on the street or at a festival.' Passion is key!

Innovation is also important. Social media is the modus operandi for the modern food truck; it's unlikely the movement would have existed without it. These days most owners are active on a range of media: Facebook, Twitter, Instagram and even specially designed smartphone apps. Savvy truck owners also allocate a generous amount of their budget to 'dress' or wrap their vehicles with eye-catching and unique designs or branding.

The variety of actual vehicles that roam the streets is also noteworthy. There are shiny Airstreams imported from the US, converted vintage caravans, Winnebagos, horse floats, vintage school buses and ex-military vehicles, making these trucks' former 'occupation' a point of interest in itself.

As a natural extension of my interests in all things urban and food related, I have to admit that it was the many innovative truck designs and the novelty of food – good food – being served out of a truck that originally caught my attention, and ignited my appetite for chasing trucks around the country. Through my research I have met so many lovely people whose unique backgrounds and various motivations I found fascinating and felt compelled to share. I hope you will enjoy delving into this small but inspiring overview into the world of food trucks.

The photographs, each with a brief introduction, showcase a lively and vibrant food movement. Accompanying the truck profiles are recipes for you to make in the comfort of your own home. The recipes represent this eclectic bunch of truck owners, bringing influences from many cultures and cuisines.

And if you happen to be in any of the Australian cities featured here, I strongly encourage you to chase down a truck or two by scanning the QR code to find out where they're next going to be serving their delicious food. Say hi from me!

ERIKA BUDIMAN

ABOUT THE AUTHOR

 Erika Budiman is an Australian graphic designer and photographer based in Melbourne with an irrepressible passion for exploring the ever-changing urban landscape.

Through her work on Explore Australia Publishing's *Hide & Seek* city guide series she had the fortune to combine work with her passion for travel, food and coffee (yes, that's a separate category!). Under the guise of work, exploring new places and meeting a diverse range of people have also become much-loved and addictive activities.

To her husband and daughter's dismay, she is one of those obsessed foodie-types who rarely visits a cafe or restaurant without first photographing the dish or the surroundings. In fact, the photography can sometimes delay a meal so much that husband and daughter have taken to counting down out loud from 10 to 0 before they descend on their food! After that all bets are off, and a carefully styled dish may suddenly become an action shot!

Thrilled to share her fascination with the exciting and growing phenomenon of food trucks all over the world, this book combines her love for design, photography and food. Erika spent close to a year chasing food trucks around Australia, and collaborated with a number of Australian food truck owners to source this diverse collection of recipes, which has turned into this stunning cookbook.

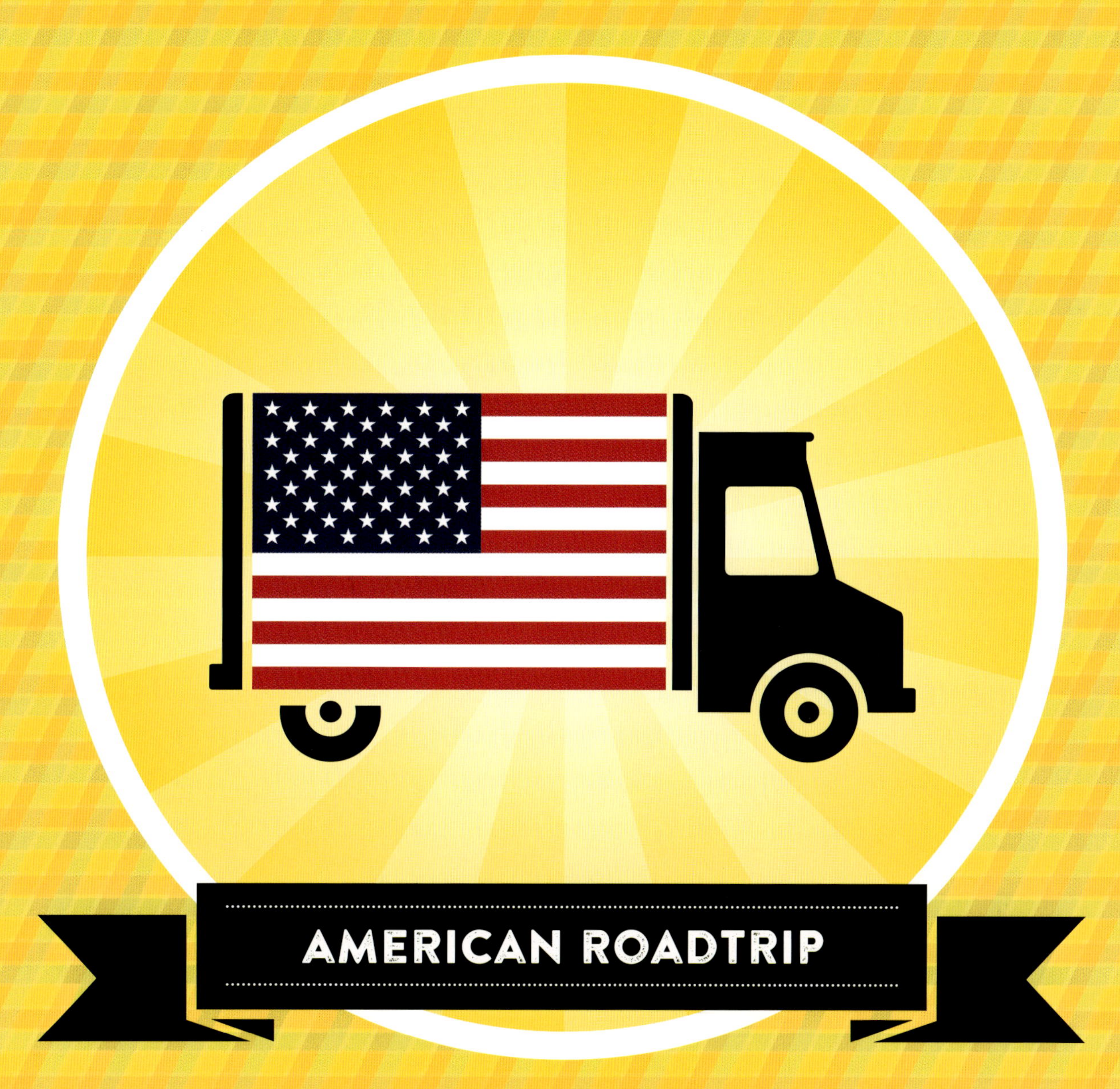

AMERICAN ROADTRIP

DUDE FOOD MAN

FRIED CHICKEN

SERVES 4

4 chicken thigh fillets
150 ml buttermilk
75 g (½ cup) plain (all-purpose) flour
60 g (½ cup) cornflour
1 tablespoon ground cumin
1 tablespoon smoked paprika
1 tablespoon ground garlic
1 tablespoon ground onion
1 tablespoon ground white pepper
1 tablespoon ground coriander
1 tablespoon salt
oil, for deep-frying

Put the chicken fillets into a saucepan and cover them with cold water. Bring to the boil then turn off the heat. Allow to sit on the stove for 10 minutes. Remove the chicken from the saucepan and pat dry.

Pour the buttermilk into a medium-size bowl. Combine the remaining ingredients (except the oil) in a separate medium-size bowl. Dip the chicken into the buttermilk and then the flour mixture.

Deep-fry the fillets at 180ºC, until golden and crispy. Place the chicken on a wire rack to remove excess oil.

Johnny, is the cool dude behind Dude Food Man truck. He was born in Istanbul, Turkey and came to Australia at age 15 where he took on an apprenticeship in the food business. He worked as a chef in high-end restaurants for ten years, specialising in French and Italian cuisine. But after starting a family he decided to become his own boss and gain full control over his business, including deciding what he cooks. And what he cooks includes full-blood wagyu beef, cold-smoked bacon, fried chicken burgers and – for the vegetarians – portobello mushroom burgers.

Johnny has served his wagyu beef burgers at large-scale music events, most recently an Alicia Keys concert, but street trading is what he loves most, where he has the time to meet and get to know his customers.

Yet life on the road does have its challenges, including competition from the growing number of food trucks and limited council permits. There are also those blustering cold and wet winters. So to help wait out the cold weather, Johnny has recently opened up a Dude Food Man diner in Melbourne, Australia.

DUDE

DUDE
Food Man
GOURMET STREET FOOD

EAT ART TRUCK

It was during a trip to the US that friends Jeremy and Mo got their first taste of the vibrant truck phenomenon. Inspired by this, they were eager to bring this innovative concept to Sydney, Australia. The two young businessmen realised their strengths lay in managing a business rather than a kitchen, so they recruited Stuart, a former sous-chef at the internationally renowned Tetsuya restaurant, and some time later Alejandro, a Cordon Bleu–trained chef from Peru. Together they created Eat Art Truck and developed a menu that's true to their ideals of serving 'progressive street food influenced by American barbecue flavours'.

With such talent on board, the expectations are high. But with a strong and loyal following, the team behind Eat Art Truck must be doing something right. The menu includes NY-style pastrami sandwiches; burger buns filled with pulled pork, barbecue beef or Cajun chicken; and kingfish ceviche (raw fish salad with lime juice) served on a bed of nachos.

As keen admirers of street art, the guys have also designated one wall of their truck as an ever-changing canvas. Each month a different local street artist is invited to paint, and then these artworks are sold off with the proceeds going to charity.

TENDER CHICKEN BITES

SERVES 4

1 kg free-range chicken thighs

MARINADE
850 g red onions, sliced
280 g garlic, crushed
580 g jalapeños
580 g shallots
50 g fresh ginger
25 g fresh thyme
50 g ground cinnamon
10 g salt
100 g chilli paste
1.5 litres (6 cups) pineapple juice
250 ml (1 cup) buttermilk

LIGHT BLUE CHEESE SAUCE
250 ml (1 cup) buttermilk
50 g white pepper
50 g (¼ cup) caster sugar
300 g blue cheese (we use Boursin blue cheese)
300 g egg-based mayonnaise

FLOUR MIXTURE
500 g ready-made pancake mix
500 g rice flour
50 g white pepper
50 g salt

Remove the excess fat from the chicken thighs and dice them into approximately 2 cm × 2 cm cubes. Rest in the refrigerator in a container or on a plate covered with plastic wrap.

To prepare the marinade, place all the ingredients, except for the pineapple juice and buttermilk, in a blender or food processor. At a low speed, blend until well combined.

In a separate bowl add the pineapple juice, buttermilk and the blended mixture. With a whisk mix them together until they are all well combined. Add the chicken thighs and marinate overnight in the refrigerator.

To make the light blue cheese sauce mix the buttermilk, white pepper and sugar in a bowl until well combined. Use your hands to crumble the blue cheese into the mix. Add the mayonnaise and mix with a spatula, folding carefully (don't blend the mixture or mix it too vigorously because the mayonnaise will heat up and may split).

Remove the chicken from the refrigerator. Strain it to remove the excess marinade. Mix all the ingredients in a bowl. Add the chicken pieces to the bowl and coat well with the flour mixture.

Preheat oil to 180ºC in a pot or deep-fryer and fry the chicken in small batches to avoid cooling down the oil.

Serve warm, with the sauce on top.

NSW EATART

GORILLA GRILL

Gorilla Grill owner Jayda was born and raised in Melbourne, Australia, after his family emigrated from Vietnam. Like many of us, Jayda began his working life at McDonald's, moving onto a range of hospitality jobs, as well as working in his parents' Vietnamese restaurant in Footscray.

Surprisingly, Jayda then gave up hospitality to work at a bank for six years, only for the call of hospitality to lure him back. It was following a trip to the United States, where he was fascinated with the bold fusion cuisine pioneered by Roy Choi's Kogi food trucks in LA, that led to Gorilla Grill the food truck. (Perhaps a blessing in disguise, as his original plans for a bricks-and-mortar eatery were blocked by developers.)

And the food truck venture seems to be treating Jayda well. Gorilla Grill experiments with a variety of dishes inspired by Jayda's Asian heritage and his love of dude food, such as Korean-style tacos filled with short ribs marinated in a spicy bulgogi sauce, served with jalapeños, mayonnaise and chilli sauce, and a side of kimchi fries. You may even be lucky to try out the samba 'fried' chicken with waffles.

BARBECUE SAUCE AND PORK RIB DRY RUB

For use with any type of pork ribs, but baby back will always be best. You can use the same dry rub for beef ribs too.

MAKES ENOUGH SAUCE AND RUB TO COAT 4 BABY BACK RIBS

BARBECUE SAUCE

1 teaspoon table salt
1 teaspoon ground black pepper
500 g (2 cups) tomato sauce (ketchup)
125 g (½ cup) yellow mustard (American mustard)
125 ml (½ cup) apple cider vinegar
80 ml (⅓ cup) worcestershire sauce
60 ml (¼ cup) lemon juice
90 g (¼ cup) dark molasses
1 teaspoon hot sauce
90 g (¼ cup) honey
185 g (1 cup) dark brown sugar
3 tablespoons vegetable oil
1 medium onion, finely chopped
4 medium garlic cloves, crushed

DRY RUB

250 g (2½ cups) paprika
230 g (1¼ cups) brown sugar
130 g (1 cup) salt
50 g (½ cup) cumin
50 g (1½ cup) black pepper
25 g (¼ cup) cayenne pepper
50 g (½ cup) ground garlic
115 g (½ cup) caster sugar

The barbecue sauce is best made the night before. In a small bowl mix the salt and black pepper. In a large bowl mix the tomato sauce (ketchup), mustard, vinegar, worcestershire sauce, lemon juice, molasses, honey, hot sauce, and dark brown sugar. These ingredients only need to be roughly combined.

Over medium heat, warm the oil in a large saucepan. Add the onions and sauté until limp and translucent for approximately 5 minutes. Add the garlic and cook for another minute. Add the salt and pepper that you mixed earlier and stir for about 2 minutes to extract their flavours. Add the wet ingredients that you mixed earlier. Simmer over medium heat for 15 minutes with the lid off to thicken the sauce.

Let the sauce sit for 24 hours in a container in the refrigerator, then it can be used to baste the ribs while cooking over a grill or barbecue.

To make the rub, mix all ingredients together and then rub on the pork ribs. Cover the ribs entirely and let sit for 4 hours in the refrigerator.

Place the ribs in a roasting tray and cook in a fan-forced oven at 150°C (170°C conventional/ Gas 3) for 100 minutes. Once cooked, serve on a plate with the barbecue sauce spread thickly on top.

Store any remaining barbecue sauce in a sealed glass container and keep for up to 2 months. Also, as long as no moisture gets into the rub, any remaining rub can be stored in an airtight container for up to 6 months.

GORILLA GRILL
— EST.2014 —

GORILLA GRILL

GUMBO KITCHEN

Founded in 2011 by Michael, Patricia and Elvin, Gumbo Kitchen is one of the original and oldest food trucks to be found in Melbourne, Australia. The truck may now be slightly battered, but Gumbo Kitchen continues to serve damn-tasty Cajun and Creole dishes.

Owners Michael and Patricia spent seven weeks in New Orleans to learn the finer details of this city's diverse cuisine. During this time they fell in love with the city's music, culture and its fierce and lively community. Gumbo Kitchen's dishes carry that same spirit with their signature gumbo containing chicken and sausage; cheesy mac croquettes; and po' boys – baguette sandwiches filled with either beef debris (gravy), fried shrimp or catfish, when it's in season.

As well as having a strong presence on the road, at festivals and events, Michael organises an annual Fat Tuesday event, better known as 'Mardi Gras', to celebrate New Orleans culture, complete with a second line parade. What's the second line, you ask? Well, in New Orleans the first line is usually made up of a brass band, while the second line is the name given to the people who walk alongside the musicians in a parade, enjoying the music and festivities.

FRIED CHICKEN AND ANDOUILLE GUMBO

In Louisiana, gumbo is made to match the local seasonal produce. Chicken and andouille smoked sausage gumbo is a classic. It is a rustic and bold gumbo recipe.

The roux is also known as Cajun napalm, so be very very careful not to splash it on yourself. When whisking the roux, be gentle and try not to change direction when stirring. Do not let it stick to the bottom of the pot. And if it burns, throw it out and start again.

SERVES 10

CHICKEN STOCK

4 chicken carcass
4 onion, diced
4 carrot, peeled and diced
3–4 celery leaves
2 garlic cloves
4 litres (16 cups) water
6 bay leaves
1 tablespoon thyme
a small handful peppercorns

1 kg chicken thigh fillets, roughly diced
salt, pepper and flour, for coating the chicken

ROUX

350 ml canola oil (do not use butter; canola oil has a higher smoking point)
350 g (2⅓ cups) plain (all-purpose) flour

2 onions, diced into medium-size chunks
2 green chillies, seeded and finely diced
5 celery stalks, diced into medium-sized chunks
2 green capsicums, seeded and finely diced
3 garlic cloves, crushed
1½ tablespoons salt
2 teaspoons ground black pepper
1 teaspoon cayenne pepper
1 teaspoon ground white pepper
4 teaspoons smoked paprika (use only good quality, as it will affect the flavour)
2 teaspoons fresh thyme
1 teaspoon dried oregano
800 g andouille sausage, sliced
1 lemon, juiced
3 litres (12 cups) chicken stock

To make the chicken stock, roast the chicken carcass with the onion, carrot, celery leaves and garlic in a fan-forced oven for 1 hour at 270ºC (290ºC conventional/Gas 9). Pour into a pot with the water, bay leaves, thyme and whole peppercorns. Bring to the boil, salt to taste and simmer for 3 hours.

Coat the chicken fillets in salt, pepper and flour. Shake off any excess flour. Heat the oil in a large soup pot. Brown the chicken until golden brown for about 2 minutes, then remove and dry using paper towels.

Next, make the roux. This takes a lot of practise to perfect. Add the flour to the oil and whisk gently. Be careful not to burn yourself. As your roux develops it should smell like roasted popcorn. As the roux darkens gradually lower the temperature. *Important note: a roux will catch on fire if left unattended.*

Once the roux is dark brown, add the onions. Make sure you stand back when you add the onions because the heat and steam that comes off the roux is incredibly hot. Cook onions for 5 minutes, until they are translucent. Add the chillies, celery and capsicum. Lower the temperature and cook for 5 minutes. Add the garlic, salt and spices and mix well using a wooden spoon.

Slowly add 1 litre (4 cups) of the chicken stock, and stir through so it is well combined. Reduce the temperature and cook for 5 minutes. Add the andouille sausage and cook for 5 minutes. Return the fried chicken to the pot, bring to the boil, and then simmer until the chicken starts to fall apart.

Add the lemon juice, taste and season with salt as required. Simmer for 1½ hours.

After simmering, skim off all the excess oil that rises to the top. The gumbo is finished when oil no longer rises to the surface.

Serve with freshly cooked long grain white rice, fresh French bread and flat-leaf parsley.

Gumbo is always better the second day, so make sure you have plenty of leftovers.

Enjoy the Cajun life and *laissez les bons temps roulette* (let the good times roll)!

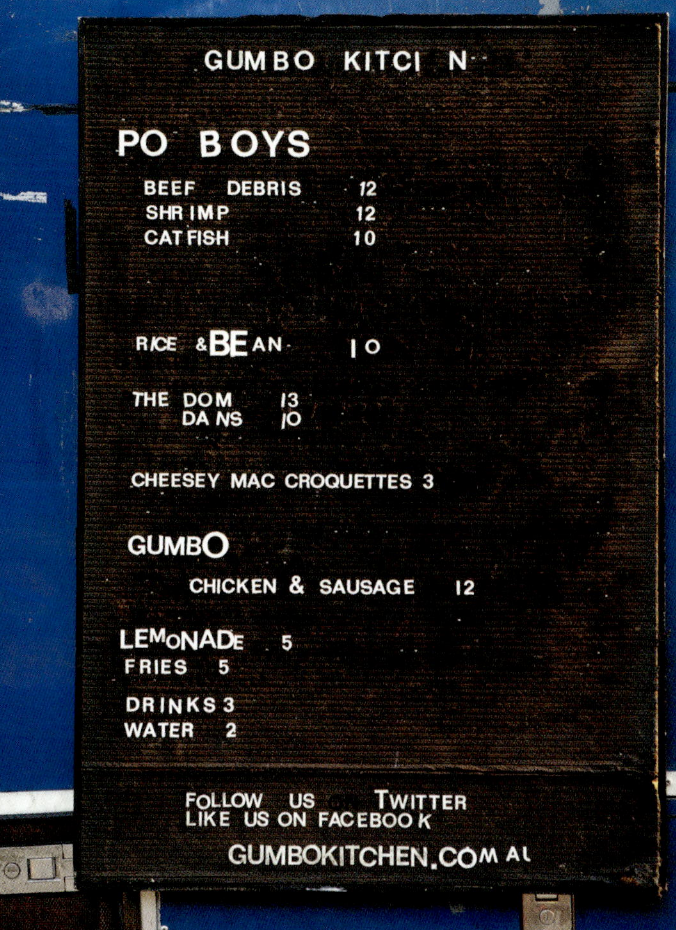

GUMBO KITCI N
PO BOYS
BEEF DEBRIS 12
SHRIMP 12
CATFISH 10
RICE & BEAN 10
THE DOM 13
DANS 10
CHEESEY MAC CROQUETTES 3
GUMBO
CHICKEN & SAUSAGE 12
LEMONADE 5
FRIES 5
DRINKS 3
WATER 2
FOLLOW US TWITTER
LIKE US ON FACEBOOK
GUMBOKITCHEN.COM AU

LOWDOWN
STREET
ORCHESTRA

Crystal
Extra Hot
Crystal

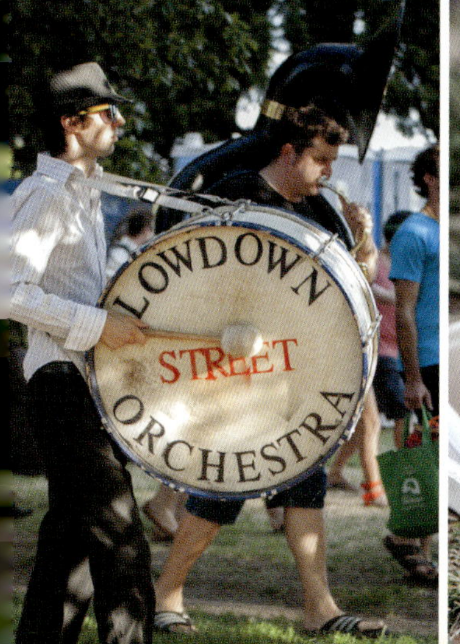

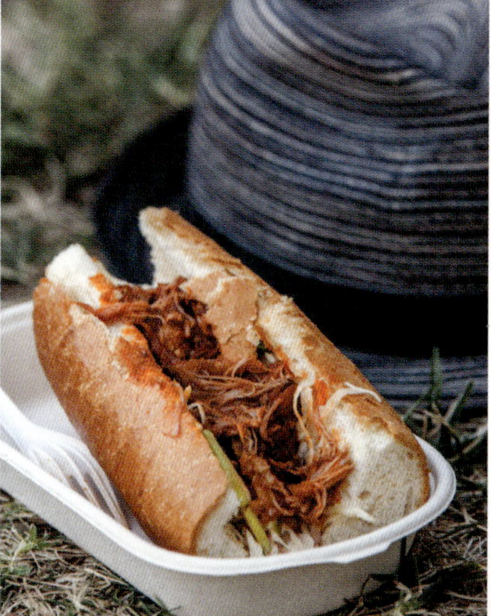

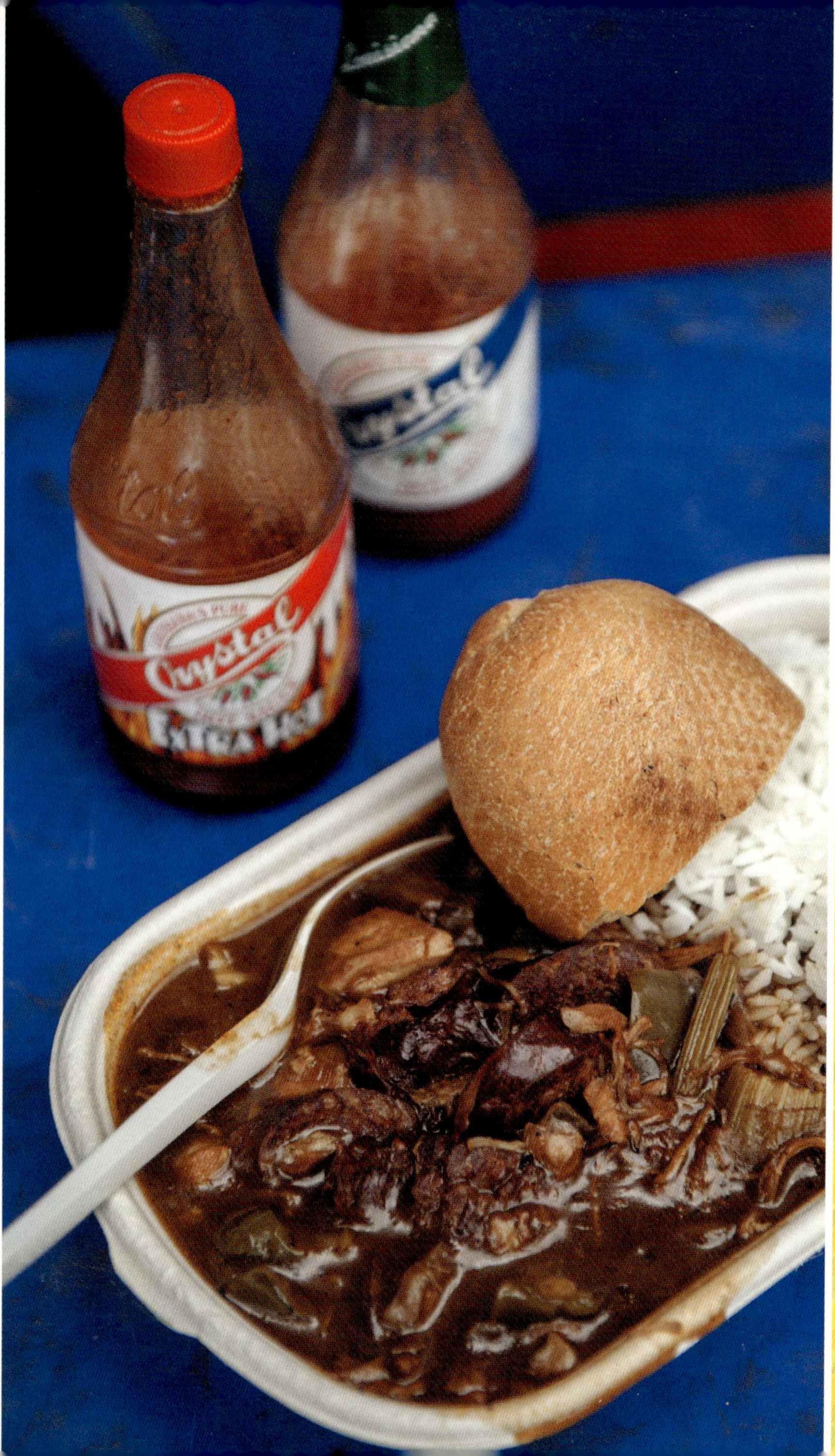

012
GUMBO KITCHEN

PO' BOY QUARTER
PO' BOYS
DEEP FRIED SHRIMP 12
SMOKED PULLED PORK 12
BEEF DEBRIS 12
FRIED GREEN TOMATO 12

PO' BOY QUARTER
PO' BOYS
DEEP FRIED SHRIMP 12
SMOKED PULLED PORK 13
BEEF DEBRIS 12
FRIED GREEN TOMATO 12

LOW & SLOW AMERICAN BBQ

For the two young owners of Low & Slow American BBQ, Angus H. and Angus K., it was their travels in North Carolina, Texas and Kansas that fuelled (pun intended) their passion for slow-cooked barbecue. Returning home they bought their rickety caravan and sold cheese toasties to save up money to purchase their first barbecue.

The converted retro caravan may be a little rickety and dusty, but whatever it lacks in style, they make up for in finger-licking sticky flavour. Originally the boys used an American-style cylinder smoker, but they have since built their own backyard barbecue pit to smoke and roast larger quantities of their meats. The menu includes slow-cooked beef brisket and pulled pork served in brioche rolls, along with regularly changing sides like apple coleslaw, potato salad, smoked corn on the cob, Texas smoked baked beans and more. They also make their own barbecue sauces and pickles.

ALL-PURPOSE RUB

Angus and Angus like to call this little number the Colonel's Secret 11. Due to copyright law, they decided against that! This rub can be used on any meat that works well in slow- or dry-cooking, i.e. roasting in a barbecue, on a charcoal grill or on a rotisserie spit. This rub works particularly well on smoked, pulled pork or roast/charcoal chicken.

MAKES ENOUGH FOR A 4 KG ROAST

185 g (1 cup) brown sugar
160 g (½ cup) kosher salt or pink salt (table salt will make the rub unpalatably salty, so try to find these salts)
4 tablespoons freshly cracked black pepper
1 tablespoon white pepper
2 tablespoons chipotle powder*
2 tablespoons paprika/smoked paprika (for a mild rub) or cayenne pepper (for a hot rub)
2 tablespoons ground mustard
3 tablespoons garlic powder
3 tablespoons onion powder
2 tablespoons dried parsley
2 tablespoons dried oregano

In a large bowl, combine all ingredients and mix together very thoroughly.

Taste it; it will be intense, but try to look past those strong flavours and look for a balance between sweet, spice and salt. This balance is what will give you a great rub. If you think it's lacking something, throw something in to find the balance that suits you.

You can store this rub in an airtight container indefinitely. The brown sugar tends to cake up after a day or so. Make sure to de-clump it and mix it thoroughly before each use.

** Chipotle powder is available from specialty food stores.*

LOW
SLOW
AMERICAN-B

LOW
SLOW
AMERICAN-BBQ

PIT COOKED
BAR-B-QUE

L&S

PAPA'S GOURMET HOTDOGS

APPLE 'N' CABBAGE 'SLAW

SERVES 4 AS A MAIN DISH OR 12 AS A SIDE DISH

¼ or ½ green cabbage
⅛ red cabbage
2 carrots, peeled
small handful of fresh parsley
5 granny smith or pink lady apples, unpeeled

DRESSING

2 tablespoons olive oil
2 tablespoons apple cider vinegar
2 tablespoons juice of fresh lime
2 tablespoons mayonnaise (we prefer Kewpie mayonnaise*)
2 teaspoons salt
2 teaspoons caster sugar

Grate the green and red cabbage into a large salad or mixing bowl. Grate the carrots and add them to the bowl. Finely chop a pinch of parsley and add it to the bowl. Cut the apples into thin slices, discarding the core. Add them to the bowl.

Add the olive oil, apple cider vinegar, juice of lime, mayonnaise, salt and sugar to the 'slaw and mix well.

** Kewpie mayonnaise is a brand of Japanese mayonnaise, and is available in the Asian foods aisle of supermarkets.*

Papa's Gourmet Hotdogs owners Jack and Nick are friends who met at university, each having come to Australia from Asia to complete their tertiary studies. When they graduated, a downturn in the Australian economy left both overqualified and unemployed, so these friends decided to create their own jobs.

As international students in Adelaide, they both grew to love the humble Aussie sausage, often served like a hotdog. And as Adelaide is brimming with fresh local produce, Jack and Nick cleverly saw a window of opportunity to serve Aussie sausages in gourmet form.

Named for when Jack became a father, Papa's Gourmet Hotdogs roams the streets of Adelaide in a replica silver Airstream that was custom-built for them in the UK. On arrival it was deemed so shiny, the boys had to change their logo to lessen the shiny surface! The menu is an easy-to-follow table of ingredients divided into types of bread, 'snags' (sausages), toppings and sauces. At AUD$8 a hotdog, there are plenty of opportunities to come back for different combinations.

SA
PAPAS

GOURMET
TRADE
Papas
MARK
HOTDOGS

GOURMET
Papas
HOTDOGS

ROUND THE WAY BAGELS

The bagel brothers, Peter and Ryan, first met ten years ago when Ryan took a job at Peter's cafe. While they may not be brothers by blood, good timing and a strong friendship led them to create this unique truck serving bagels.

A former off-road mountain-boarder, once ranked eleventh in the world, Ryan came to love bagels while on a trip through the Czech Republic. Peter, a qualified chef with a European background, has always had a passion for simple but good-quality food. Both of them happened to be seeking a change of scenery at the same time, so they decided to spice up an oversaturated burger market with the simple bagel.

Their NY-inspired Reuben pastrami bagel/burger is an absolute must, but there are other fantastic options like the 'Czech 1–2' that uses ćevapi sausage and the 'Chan Chan' containing chicken breast marinated in spiced Cuban rum.

CHAN CHAN BAGEL/BURGER

Chicken breast marinated in spiced Cuban rum with chimichurri, lettuce, tomato and tangy mayonnaise.

Usually the boys would use their own Chan Chan sauce, but since our recipe is a secret here's a good alternative – and it's good, just not as good as our Chan Chan sauce!

SERVES 1

CHIMICHURRI PASTE
1 bunch fresh parsley
1 bunch spring onions
2 garlic cloves
100 ml olive oil
1 lime, zest and juice
splash of balsamic vinegar

pinch of turmeric
pinch of paprika
pinch of ground cumin
small handful fresh coriander leaves, torn
spiced Cuban rum (enough to cover the chicken)
600 ml Coca-Cola

CHAN CHAN SAUCE ALTERNATIVE
30 ml American mayonnaise
10 ml hot sauce of your choice (we prefer green Tabasco sauce)

1 chicken breast
1 bagel
2–3 cos lettuce leaves
1 tomato, sliced

To prepare the chimichurri paste, wash the parsley and spring onions. Trim the ends off the parsley and the green leaves off the spring onions, and put in a blender. Clean the garlic cloves and put in the blender. Blend until a paste forms. Add the olive oil, lime zest and a splash of balsamic vinegar. Taste.

In a medium-size bowl mix the turmeric, paprika, cumin and coriander leaves. Put the chicken into the bowl and coat thickly with the spices. Pour the Cuban rum and Coca-Cola over the chicken until covered. Leave to marinate for 2 hours.

To make the Chan Chan sauce alternative, mix the American mayonnaise with your choice of hot sauce.

On a hot plate, grill the chicken breast for a few minutes on each side. Brush with the chimichurri paste whilst cooking.

Slice the bagel in half and toast to your liking. Spread the inside of one half of the toasted bagel with the Chan Chan sauce alternative. Then top with the cos lettuce leaves, a few slices of tomato and the chicken. Cover with the lid and eat!

Round
the Way
BAGEL BURGERS

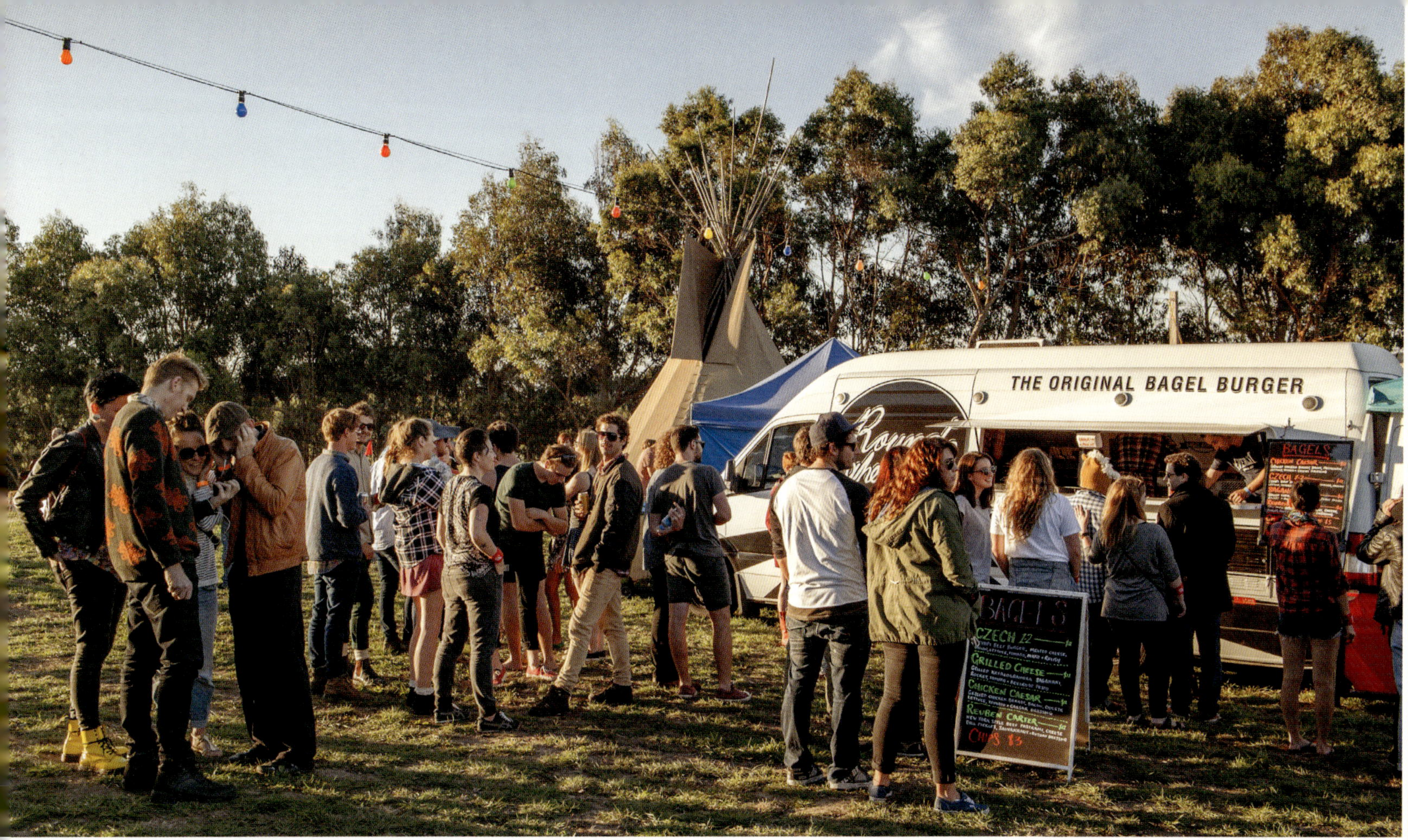

THE ORIGINAL BAGEL BURGER
Round the Way
BAGEL BURGERS

SLIDERS ON TYRES

It took chief slider Owen a bit of convincing, on his wife Emily's part, to believe that a food truck would be a better business venture than the bricks-and-mortar eatery he'd been eyeing off. Owen had worked as a chef in the fine-dining industry for more than ten years, with positions held in high-end restaurants including Vue De Monde, owned by well-known Australian chef Shannon Bennett. Owen even had a brief stint in Australia's parliament canteen cooking for prime minister John Howard. But since Owen was finally convinced, he's not regretting his choice to start up Sliders on Tyres.

Hitting the roads of Melbourne, Australia in 2013, Owen has been able to utilise his finely tuned cooking skills and passion for restaurant-quality, American-style 'fast' foods. The food truck offers mini sliders that come with either pulled lamb, Spanish sausage or spiced calamari, served on mini-brioche buns with specially made dressings. Occasionally there may also be a soft-shell crab slider on offer and in summer you may be treated to a coconut and tapioca pudding served with mango, lime and honey.

SOFT-SHELL CRAB SLIDERS WITH PICKLED CUCUMBER AND TOMATO SALAD, SAFFRON AND LEMON MAYONNAISE

MAKES 6 SLIDERS

PICKLED CUCUMBERS

2 continental cucumbers, thinly sliced
half bunch fresh dill
6 black peppercorns
1 bunch thyme
1 brown onion, thinly sliced
250 ml (1 cup) water
1 star anise
250 ml (1 cup) white wine vinegar
25 g caster sugar

SAFFRON AND LEMON MAYONNAISE

3 threads saffron
1 tablespoon hot water
3 egg yolks
1 teaspoon smoked parika
1 tablespoon white vinegar
1 tablespoon dijon mustard
1 lemon, juiced and zested
500 ml (2 cups) light olive oil

SHALLOW-FRIED SOFT-SHELL CRAB

3 soft-shell crabs (cleaned)
250 g (2 cups) cornflour
2 teaspoons salt

1 bunch baby cos lettuce
2 ripe tomatoes
splash of lemon juice
half bunch chives
6 mini brioche buns, cut in half

It's best to prepare the cucumbers at least 1 week earlier to give them time to pickle. To prepare the pickled cucumbers, layer the cucumber alternating with the dill, peppercorns, thyme and onion in a clean, dry 1 litre jar. Combine the water, star anise, vinegar and sugar in a medium-size saucepan. Bring to the boil over medium–high heat, then carefully pour the hot liquid over the ingredients in the jar. Seal the jar immediately. Store the jar at room temperature until opened (refrigerate after opening).

To make the saffron and lemon mayonnaise, place the saffron and hot water in a small cup and set aside for 10 minutes to soak. Place the egg yolks, smoked paprika, vinegar, mustard, lemon juice and zest, and saffron water in a food processor and process until frothy. While the motor is running, gradually add the oil in a thin, steady stream and process until the mixture thickens. Season with salt and pepper. Transfer to an airtight container and refrigerate.

Next, prepare the soft-shell crab. If using fresh crabs, make sure you clean them correctly by removing the lungs. Combine the salt and cornflour in a large bowl. Add your soft-shell crabs to the cornflour mixture and coat heavily. Heat the oil in a frying pan over medium heat to around 165ºC (using a cooking thermometer). Shallow fry the crabs for 2 minutes on each side. Remove and place on absorbent paper towel to remove excess oil. Cut each crab in half.

To make the pickled cucumber and tomato salad, place the pickled cucumbers in a salad bowl. Quarter the tomatoes, removing the seeds, and slice them thinly. Add them to the salad bowl. Mix the dill cucumber pickle and tomatoes together, adding the lemon juice and salt to taste. Cut the chives into long pieces and mix through the salad.

To assemble the sliders cut the buns in half lengthways and grill on the inside for 1 minute, until brown.

Place a teaspoon of mayonnaise on each inside of the brioche buns. On the bottom half of each bun place a tablespoon of the salad then top with half a crab. Place the bun lids on top, finishing the sliders with bamboo skewers (available at most supermarkets).

SLiDERS ON TYRES
Awesome street food on the move!
SLiDERS ON TYRES

Sliders
on TYRES
AWESOME STREET FOOD ON THE MOVE!

Sliders
on TYRES

EST 2013
Sliders
on TYRES

SMOKIN' BARRYS

BBQ RUB

Accoring to Smokin' Barrys this is a good, sweet brisket rub that can also be used for pork or chicken. Of course, you can adjust the heat by using mild or hot chilli powder.

MAKES ENOUGH FOR APPROXIMATELY 2–3 KG OF BEEF BRISKET

60 g (⅓ cup) brown sugar
105 g (⅓ cup) salt (coarse salt works best)
35 g (⅓ cup) Hungarian paprika
35 g (⅓ cup) chilli powder (choose a mild or hot powder,
   depending on your taste)
35 g (⅓ cup) ground black pepper

Mix all ingredients together in a large bowl.

Use 1 cup of the rub to pack firmly around the brisket. Cover with plastic wrap or remove from the bowl and place in a large plastic bag, and allow to marinate in the refrigerator for 12–24 hours before cooking using your preferred method.

This rub can be stored in an airtight container for several days, but after a week or two the brown sugar will crystallise.

Put away your knives and forks, this is finger-licking Smokin' Barry style! And we can just imagine the happy mess Smokin' Barrys food will leave you in, as truck owner Jim proudly proclaims 'you don't need teeth' to eat his meat!

Jim's love of barbecue developed during a year-long trip around Australia in a caravan with a Foxtel box. Jim indulged in nightly viewings of food shows, and from this began his self-made school of American barbecue.

Smokin' Barrys food is dude food at its best, bringing together American and Australian barbecue cultures. There are succulent hickory-smoked beef and pork ribs, or a number of pulled-pork and beef rolls with apple 'slaw. Depending on what topping combination you choose (select from the likes of jalapeños, guacamole, sour cream and Tabasco), you may be chomping down on a 'Barry Manilow', 'Barry Gibb' (one of the Bee Gees), 'Barry Humphries' (the man behind comedian Dame Edna Everage) or 'Drew Barrymore' – which are just some of the Barry-named roll combinations. Upsize your dude food experience with an order of chilli fries.

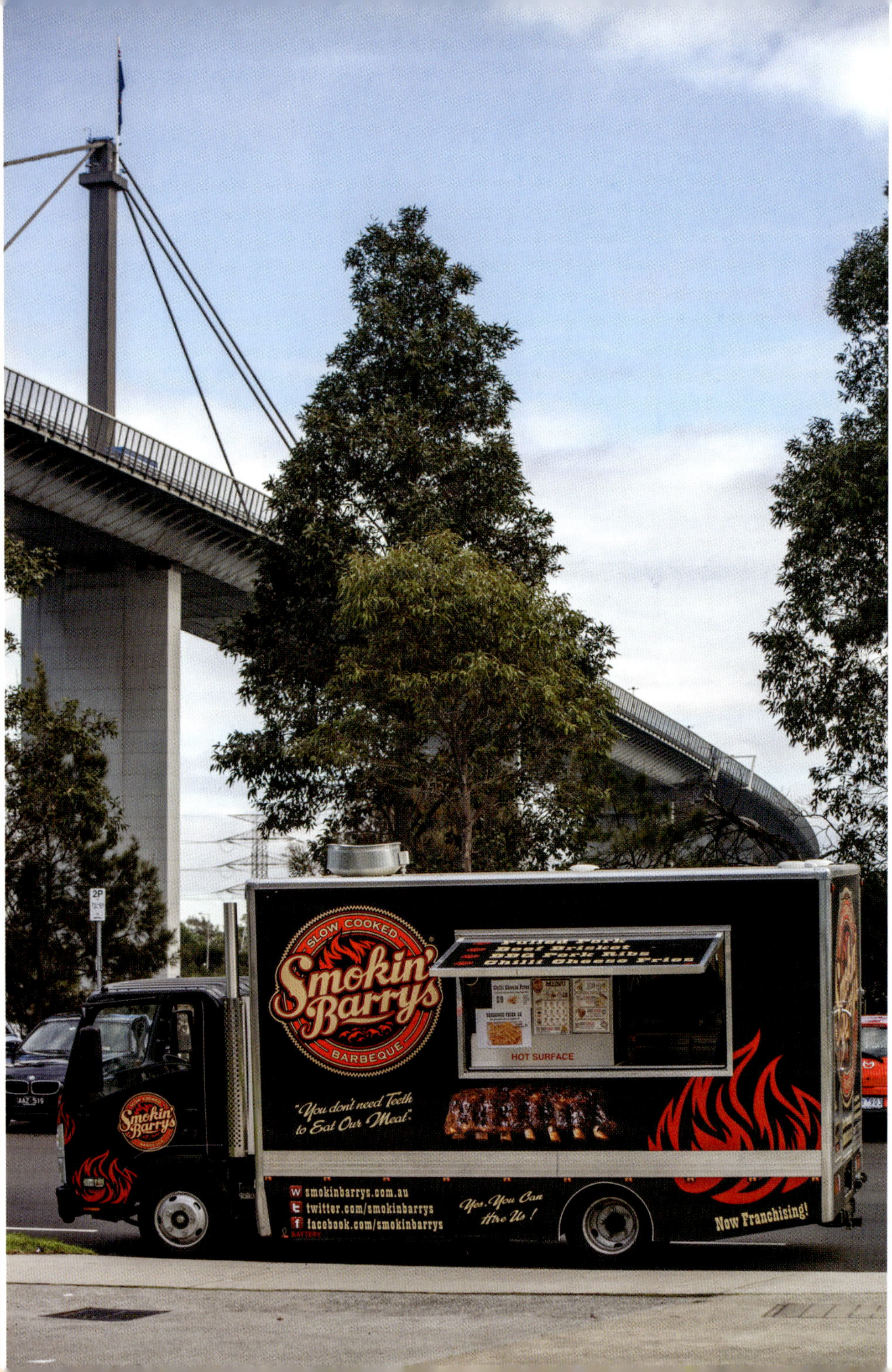

Smokin'
Barrys
SLOW COOKED
BARBEQUE
"You don't need Teeth
to Eat Our Meat"
HOT SURFACE

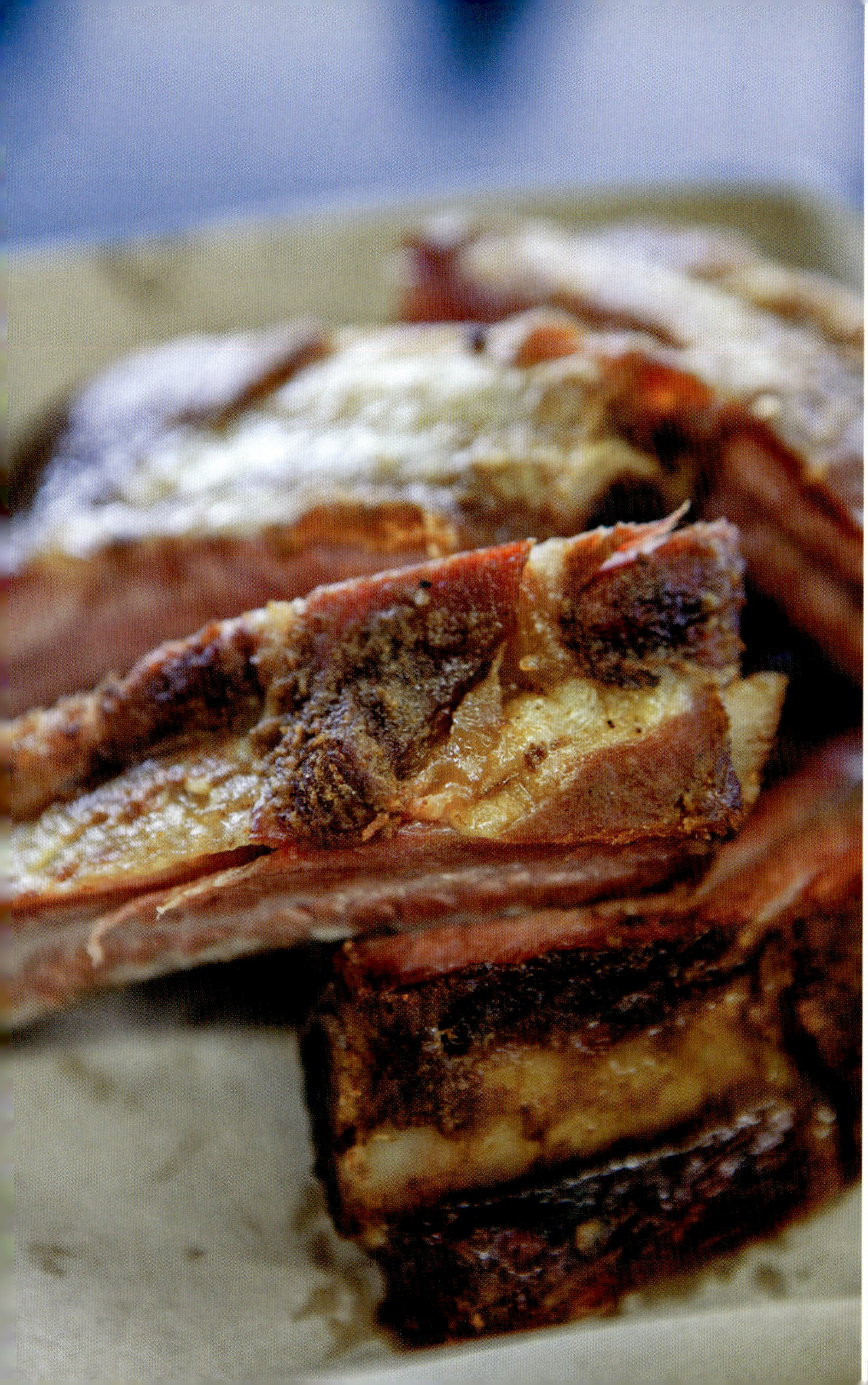

SLOW COOKED
Now Franchising!
0409 60 18 10

Smokin' Barry's

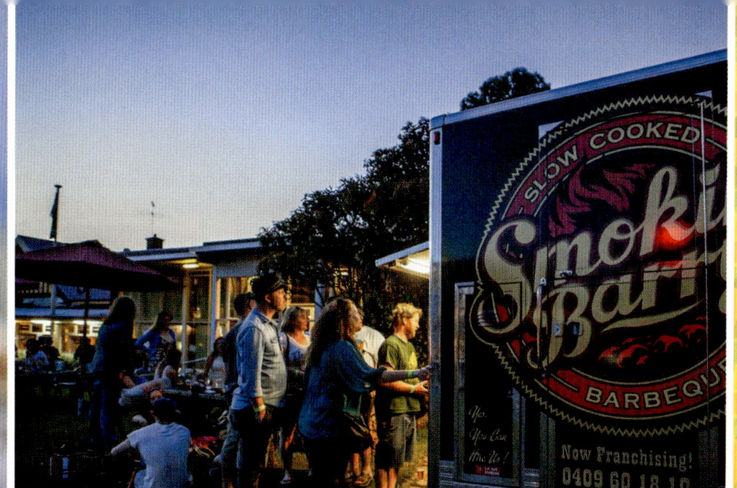

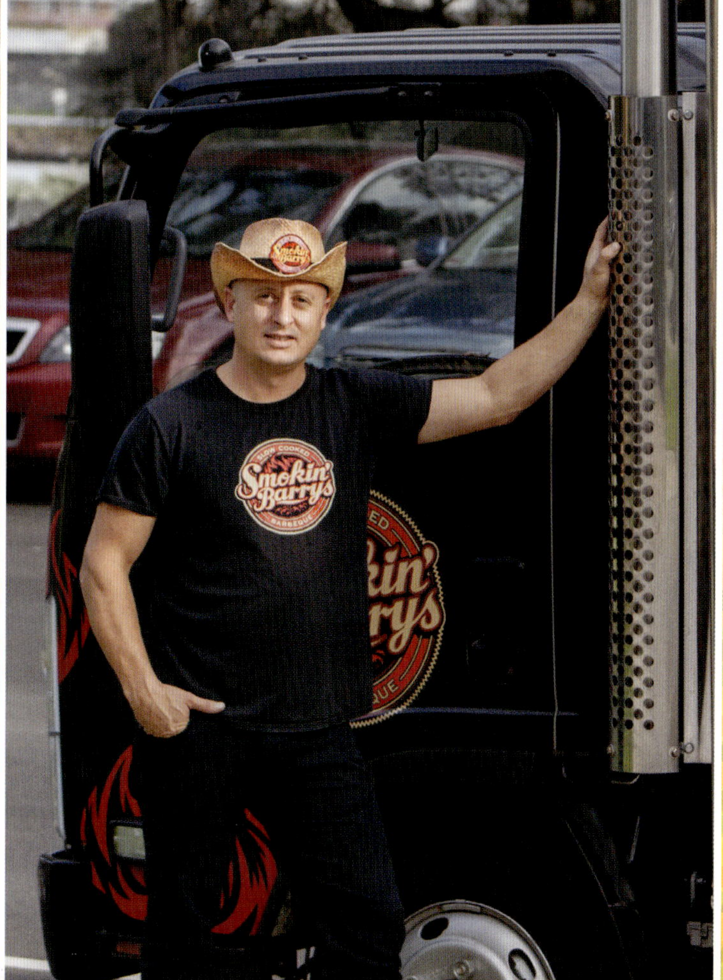

SNEAKY PICKLE

BREAD AND BUTTER PICKLES

MAKES 3 CUPS

CUCUMBERS
6 baby cucumbers, sliced (use crinkle cutter if possible)
1 tablespoon pickling salt
135 g (1 cup) ice cubes

200 g (1 cups) caster sugar
1 teaspoon turmeric
1 teaspoon celery salt
2 teaspoons yellow mustard seeds
375ml (1½ cups) apple cider vinegar

Put the cucumbers in a bowl. Sprinkle with salt. Place the ice cubes on top, cover with plastic wrap and leave on a benchtop for 3–4 hours. Wash cucumbers thoroughly under cold water and drain.

Place all other ingredients in a pot and bring to the boil. Remove from the heat.

Place the well-drained cucumbers in clean jars. Pour the hot liquid into each jar, covering the cucumbers and filling the jars. Allow to cool.

Once cooled place lids on jars and refrigerate. Use within 4–5 weeks. We recommend using these pickles in sandwiches or with meat platters.

The husband and wife team behind Sneaky Pickle food truck, Jeff and Amanda, are nothing if not passionate about food. In fact, Jeff is truly in his element when he talks about their favourite cuisine, American-style sandwiches and slow-cooked barbecue.

Most of Jeff's cooking experience has been in the fine-dining industry, while Amanda has worked in pubs and bistros. Together they spent extensive time travelling through the States, tasting and learning about the fine art of American sandwiches, barbecue and smoking. The result is Sneaky Pickle's delicious sandwiches and burgers, using juicy meat that requires at least 2 hours of brining (soaked in a mixture of salt and sugar), followed by 10–12 hours of slow cooking. The couple uses an American vertical smoker to slow-cook meats such as brisket, pastrami and pulled pork. Several racks of meat are stacked on top of each other in the smoker to ensure that none of the delicious juices are wasted.

Their homemade sneaky pickles are a perfect accompaniment to their slow-cooked meats, balancing the rich meat with a pleasant hit of acid. The menu also regularly mixes it up with shrimp po' boys, pulled-pork buns, chilli or jalapeño poppers (not to mention the sweet pies!). And if you're lucky enough to see this food truck at a festival, make sure to try one of their special turkey legs that come out just for the occasion. Served whole, with only a strip of aluminum around the bone and no dignifying plate or cutlery in sight, these turkey legs demand you summon your inner Flintstone to fully enjoy them in an unadulterated fashion.

STREET SLIDERS

One of the benefits of a mobile food business is the variety it offers. Where you trade today, may not be where you trade tomorrow. Under this motto, Mauritian-born siblings Patrice and Natalie were surprised to find themselves catering a 21st birthday party for Australian Prime Minister Tony Abbott's daughter. Having dealt with 'Margie' (Mrs Abbott) until the day of the event, they didn't realise until they arrived at the address that this wasn't just any Mrs Abbott!

Of course, you don't get these sorts of gigs without having a good name and products to match. With a vintage American bus that used to be hired out for film sets, the siblings have developed a tight American-diner-style menu featuring sliders of all kinds. There are gourmet mini burgers filled with pulled pork, grilled chicken or beef patties, as well as hand-cut fries and corn on the cob. In summer, they also bring out American-style shakes such as strawberry buttermilk and blueberry, or something a little more unconventional like their avocado and lemon shake.

PRIME SLIDER

Beef patty, roasted tomato, maple-caramalised bacon, braised onions, shaved iceberg lettuce, aged cheddar melt

SERVES 4

HOMEMADE MAYONNAISE

5 egg yolks
2 tablespoons mustard
1 lemon, juiced
700 ml olive oil

BRAISED ONIONS

2 large brown onions, sliced
1 tablespoon oil

MAPLE-CARAMELISED BACON

100 g (½ cup) brown sugar
1 tablespoon hot water
75 ml maple syrup
2 rashers bacon, cut in half

ROASTED TOMATOES

2 tomatoes, halved

4 brioche slider buns
200 g lean beef mince
4 slices cheddar cheese (we prefer aged cheddar for extra tang)
handful iceberg lettuce, shredded

Make the mayonnaise first. Combine the egg yolks, mustard and lemon juice in a large bowl of a food processor. Gradually add the oil while continuing to mix the other ingredients, until well combined. Add salt to taste.

Next, make the braised onions. Coat the bottom of a small saucepan with oil. Add the onions and sauté; start on a high flame, stirring well. After a few minutes add salt and lower the flame. Cool until aromatic and evenly coloured. Adjust seasoning to your liking.

To make the maple-caramelised bacon place the brown sugar and maple syrup in a small saucepan and heat over a very low flame until the sugar has dissolved. Allow to cool. Mix 1 tablespoon of the sugar mixture with the hot water. Brush the mixture over the bacon and fry until nicely coloured.

To prepare the roasted tomatoes, core the tomatoes and quarter them lengthways. Scoop out the seeds and discard. Place the tomatoes on a baking tray, skin side down. Spray or pour olive oil evenly over the tomatoes and season with salt. Bake in a fan-forced oven at 220°C (240°C conventional/Gas 8) for 10–20 minutes, until they are almost caramelised and crispy at the edges. Remove from oven and allow to cool.

Now it's time to build the slider! Toast the brioche buns until slightly crispy. Spread the base with a teaspoon of the homemade mayonnaise.

Divide the mince into 4 portions and form into patties. On a hot plate (or similar) grill one side of the patties for a few minutes. Flip them and place a small amount of braised onions and a piece of maple-caramelised bacon on top of each patty. Place the cheese on top of the bacon and continue to cook so that the cheese melts over the patties.

Transfer patties to brioches bases, top with the iceberg lettuce and roasted tomato. Cover with brioche lid and enjoy!

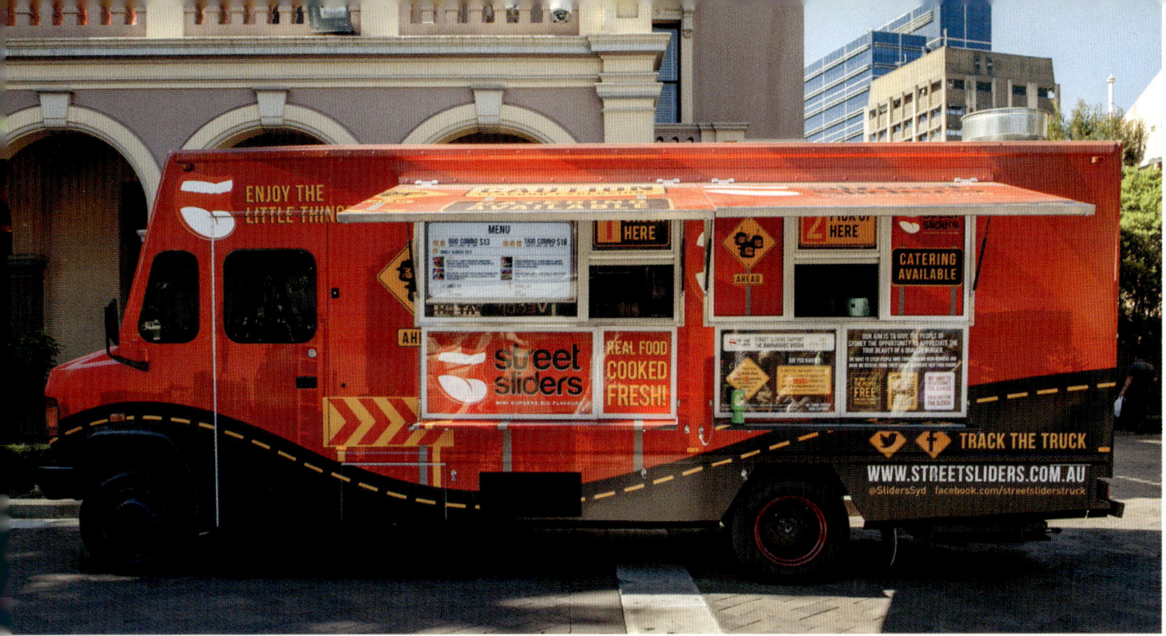
ENJOY THE
street sliders
REAL FOOD COOKED FRESH!
CATERING AVAILABLE
TRACK THE TRUCK
WWW.STREETSLIDERS.COM.AU
@SlidersSyd facebook.com/streetsliderstruck

MAKE WAY FO
THE SLIDER

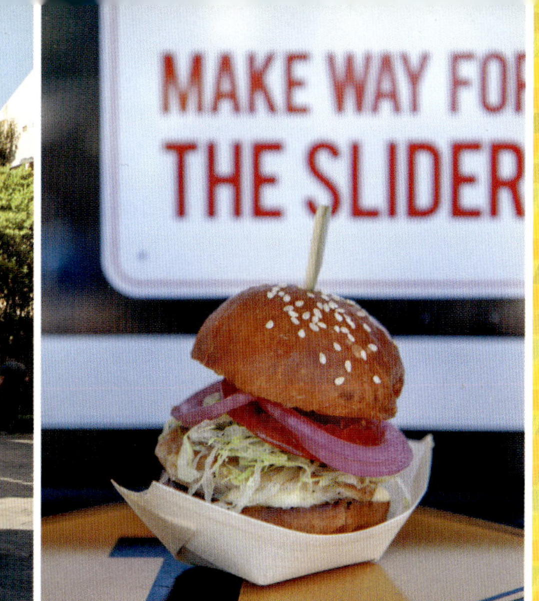

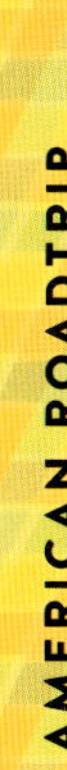

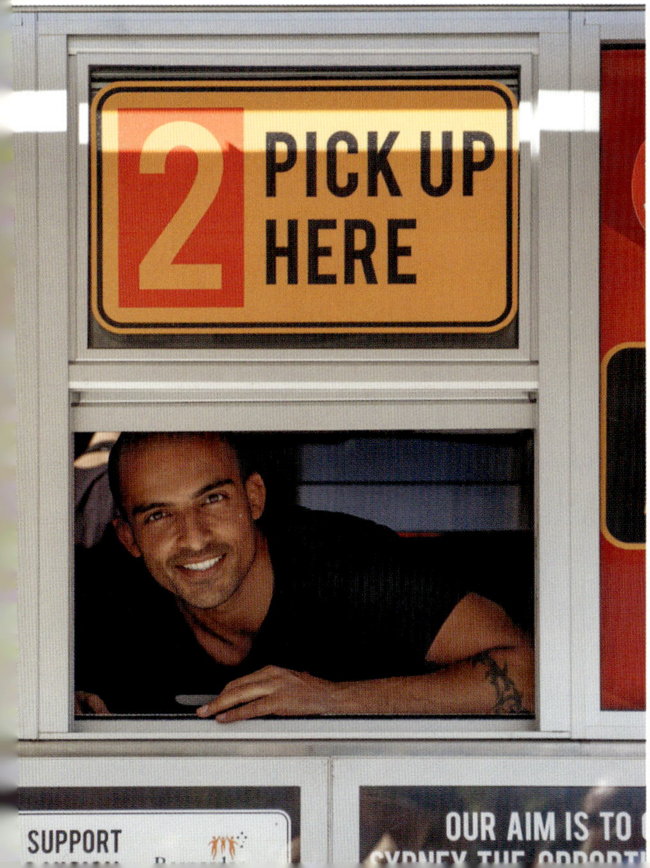
2 PICK UP HERE
SUPPORT
OUR AIM IS TO

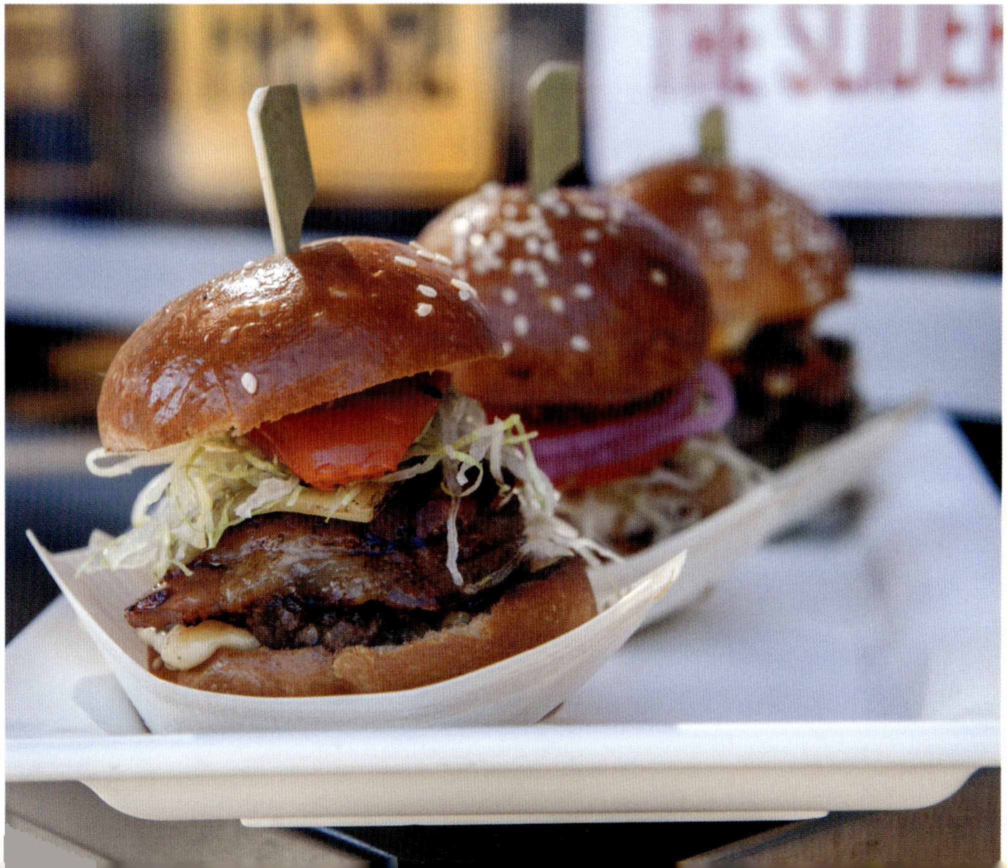

Asian adventures

BÁNH MÌ BOYS

The Bánh Mì Boys food truck hit the streets of Melbourne, Australia in 2013 with an eclectic team made up of Keen, a management consultant (and coincidentally also a MasterChef Australia top 30 contestant); Darren, a Chinese medicine doctor; and Francis, a lawyer. Sharing a common cultural heritage, as well as a love for Vietnamese flavours, the Bánh Mì Boys are dishing out tasty Vietnamese baguettes with a difference.

Instead of the traditional filling of thinly sliced cold cuts (usually pork), the Bánh Mì Boys' rolls are filled with a choice of either sliced pork belly, zesty chicken strips or cubes of eggplant, which come fresh and hot off the grill. Added to this are pickled carrots, cucumbers, coriander, aioli and spicy dressing to complete the roll.

The business has quickly built up a large following, nicknamed the Bánh Mì army. The boys have even served their Vietnamese baguettes and other street food items at large-scale music festivals, one of which had them working continuously for 18 hours with only two hours of sleep before it all started again the next day.

VIETNAMESE ORANGE AND GINGER CEVICHE

SERVES 6

MARINADE

4 oranges, juiced
1 lime, juiced
small knob (about a tablespoon) of ginger, finely grated

DESICCATED COCONUT

100 g desiccated coconut
2 tablespoons fish sauce
1 teaspoon sambal oelek (chilli paste)

400 g blue cod / cod / snapper fillets (we use Chatham Island blue cod)
2 tablespoons salt
12 betel leaves*

1 semi-ripe mango, finely diced
5 kaffir lime leaves, julienned

Prepare the marinade first. In a large cup combine the orange and lime juices. Add the ginger to macerate with the juices for 30 minutes before use.

To make the desiccated coconut, preheat a fan-forced oven to 150°C (170°C conventional/Gas 3). Place coconut in a large bowl and add the fish sauce and sambal oelek. Mix them together until well combined. Pour the coconut mixture onto a large flat tray lined with baking paper, and bake in the oven for 20 minutes.

Lightly rub the fish with salt and leave for 5 minutes before washing the salt off. Thinly slice the fish into sashimi-style slices and place carefully into a deep serving dish.

Pour the marinade into the deep serving dish to just cover the fish. Leave for 20 minutes. Remove the fish and evenly distribute slices onto a neat pile of betel leaves. Add a little more of the marinade on top with a few slivers of ginger.

To serve, place a small portion of mango on top of the fish, followed by some of the coconut and a sprinkling of kaffir lime leaves.

* Betel leaves are available from Asian supermarkets.

BÁNH MÌ BOYS
VIETNAMESE STREET FOOD

BÁNH MÌ BOYS
VIE MESE STREET FOOD

THE BUN MOBILE

With two trucks, one red and one blue, the Bun Mobiles roam the streets of Brisbane, Australia selling steamed Asian buns for AUD$8 a bun. That's quite a steal for these soft, pillowy steamed buns filled with either twice-cooked pork, wagyu beef or teriyaki chicken, so it's no wonder the Bun Mobile has been featured in The New York Times '36 Hours in Brisbane', as well as several international TV shows.

This food truck is a tight-knit family business, which includes couple Harry and Christine, and Christine's son Daniel with his wife Natasha. Both Harry and Daniel are qualified chefs, with Harry having trained at Le Cordon Bleu in London. The family members consult regularly to concoct new combinations for their steamed buns, including some vegetarian options.

The other benefit of their mobile business is that it gives the two couples direct contact with their customers. It's much easier to know which flavours work best when there are no middle men.

SOUS VIDE PORK BELLY

You'll need a slow cooker to create this dish. A food vacuum sealer is also helpful, although standard zip-lock bags are also sufficient.

SERVES 4–6

1 kg pork belly, (we prefer skin on because it enhances the flavour)
2 tablespoons kosher salt (you can use regular salt if necessary)
1 litre (4 cups) water

200 ml stock from sous vide pork
100 ml dark soy
100 ml usukchi shoyu*
100 ml mirin
4 star anise
1 teaspoon (heaped) five spice powder
1 tablespoon fresh ginger, chopped

steamed bun
creamy coleslaw
butter lettuce
fried shallots
sliced green onions

To prepare the pork combine the salt and water in a large container to make a brine mixture. Mix until the salt has completely dissolved. Place pork in the brine mixture. Cover and refrigerate for 12 hours.

Remove the pork from the liquid and pat dry. Place the pork into a zip-lock bag and seal, ready to sous vide.

Heat the water (enough to cover the zip-lock back) in a large pot or in a kettle to 63°C (test using a thermometer) and then pour the water into the slow cooker. Submerge the zip-lock bag with pork inside. Slow cook the pork for 24 hours. Remove the pork and rest it.

To prepare the braising liquid combine the stock, dark soy, usukchi shoyu, mirin, star anise, five spice powder and ginger in a medium-size pot. Slice the pork and place it in the braising liquid. Gently simmer over low heat for 30 minutes.

Serve the pork belly in a steamed bun, with creamy coleslaw, butter lettuce, fried shallots and sliced green onions.

** Usukchi shoyu is a lighter, saltier soy sauce, available from most Asian supermarkets.*

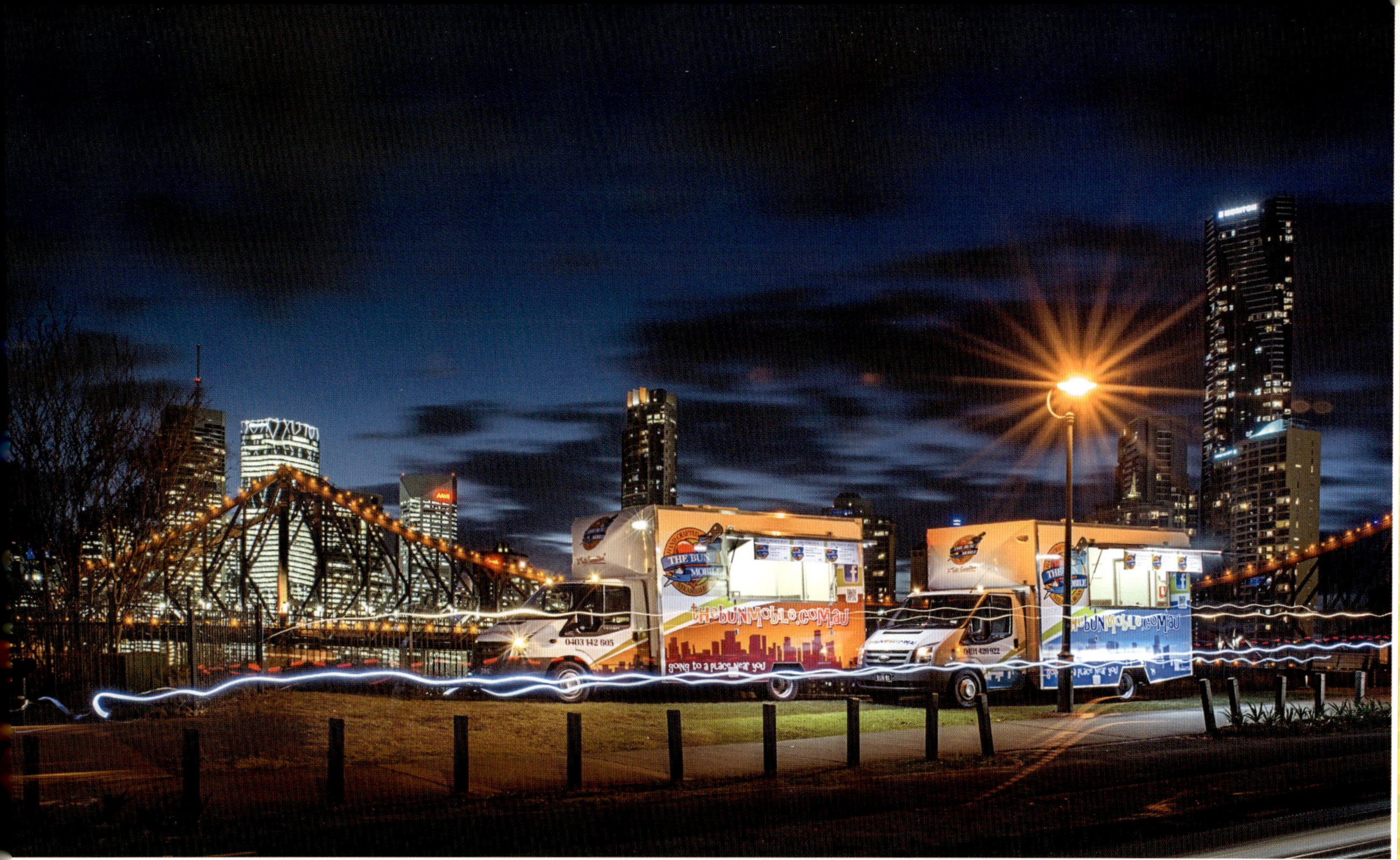
THE BUN MOBILE
thebunmobile.com.au
0403 142 605
going to a place near you
0401 420 922

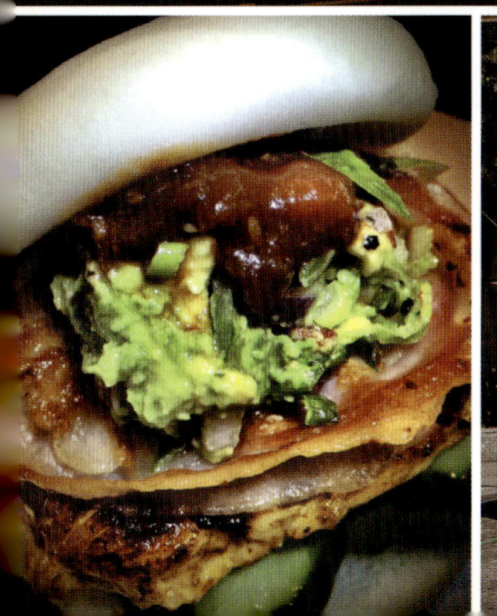

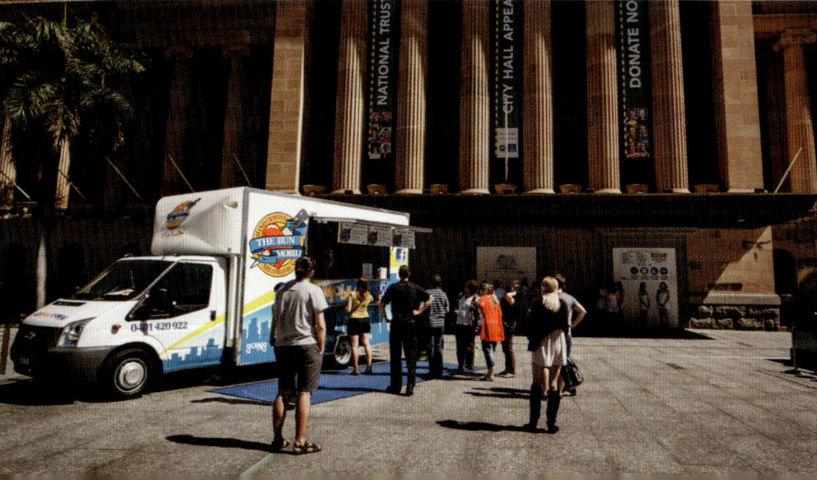

NATIONAL TRUST
CITY HALL APPEAL
DONATE NO
THE BUN MOBILE
0401 420 922

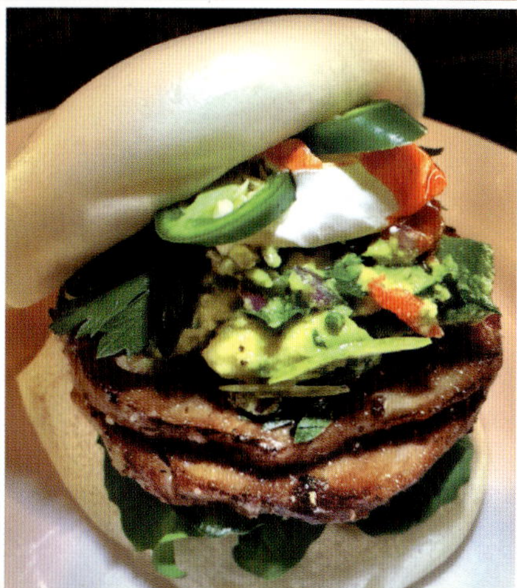

THE CURRY TRUCK

Australia is such a melting pot of cultures that a Lebanese man can surely cook good Indian curries. Unsure? Well, don't be fooled by the Taj Mahal graphic on his truck – the Curry Truck owner Ibi doesn't just cook Indian food. He has a passion for all things curry, which can range from Malaysian to Indonesian curries.

A self-confessed YouTube junkie, Ibi owes his curry making skills to fanatically studying and practising video recipes found online. Before entering the food truck world, Ibi was a security guard, but also worked as a sales rep for a large chip company, where he gained many skills that are now useful for his own business.

Ibi admits there are some downsides to his business – dealing with councils to get permits and often having poor weather to contend with – but Ibi's friendly and cheeky personality have made him a much-loved figure in the suburb of Yarraville in Melbourne, Australia. When he's not serving his delicious curries, he's likely to be playing pranks on fellow food truck amigos.

BEEF RENDANG

SERVES 4–5

PASTE

6–12 dried red chillies (depending on how hot you like it), seeded
4 medium red onions, chopped
2 lemongrass stems, chopped
10 garlic cloves
12.5 cm (5 inch) piece ginger
12.5 cm (5 inch) piece galangal

5–6 tablespoons vegetable oil
1 tablespoon curry powder
2 kg chuck beef, diced
400 ml coconut milk
3–5 tablespoons sweet soy sauce or sweet cooking caramel

To make the paste, soak the chillies in boiling water for 10 minutes. Remove the chillies from the water using a slivered spoon and put them with all other ingredients into a blender. Pour a little water from the red chillies into the blender to help the blending process. Blend until all the ingredients are combined.

Heat vegetable oil in a medium-size pot. Add the paste that you have just made and cook for 10 minutes on medium–high heat, stirring frequently.

Add the curry powder and keep stirring for another 3 minutes. Add the beef and stir until the meat browns slightly. Do not burn or overcook the meat. Add the coconut milk, then bring to the boil while continuing to stir.

Once boiling, reduce the heat to low and leave the pot uncovered. Cook for 1–1½ hours so the beef is soft and full of flavour. Stir every 20–30 minutes.

Once cooked, add the sweet soy sauce and salt to taste. Cook for a further 10 minutes to reduce liquid (this dish should not be watery or dry, but moist).

Serve with rice.

The
CURRY TRUCK

The curry Truck

GHOST KITCHEN

SPRING ONION PANCAKES

MAKES 20 PANCAKES

1 tablespoon vegetable oil
5 spring onions, finely diced
600 g (4 cups) plain (all-purpose) flour
750 ml (3 cups) warm water
1 tablespoon sesame oil

Put the oil in a large pot with half the spring onions and 100 g flour. Stir over low heat for 5 minutes. Turn off the heat and allow the mixture to cool for 20 minutes.

Add the remaining flour to the mixture, along with 1 cup of the warm water, start kneading the mixture inside the pot until a dough forms. Continue the process until the remaining 2 cups of warm water have been added.

Add the sesame oil to help remove the dough from the pot. Add the rest of the spring onions to the dough and knead to combine.

Divide the dough into palm-size balls. Sprinkle flour onto a flat working surface then using a rolling pin, roll each ball out onto the floured surface into a circular shape.

Heat a frying pan with oil and cook each pancake on both sides until golden brown.

Taiwanese-born Jenny was working as a graphic designer, when she found herself seeking a change of scene. Her grandmother taught her how to cook at a young age, so using these skills she decided to see whether there was a market for Taiwanese street food in Melbourne, Australia (answer: yes!). With a truck found on Gumtree, she then found a specialist to fit out the truck with a second-hand industrial kitchen, and commissioned street artist Ero to go crazy with colour and graphics on the exterior. And so the Ghost Kitchen food truck was born.

The name Ghost Kitchen is a nod to Jenny's cultural roots, referring to the ghost month in the Chinese calendar when people pay respect to the deceased. But the menu is anything but lifeless. There are sweet potato fries, gua bao (Taiwanese-style steamed buns filled with slow-braised pork belly, ground peanuts, pickles and coriander), salt and pepper popcorn chicken, Taiwanese sausage served on a stick, and a winter melon tea prepared by the Ghost Kitchen team.

GHOST
KITCHEN
TAIWANESE STREET FOOD
鬼廚房

Taiwanese street food to enlighten the soul

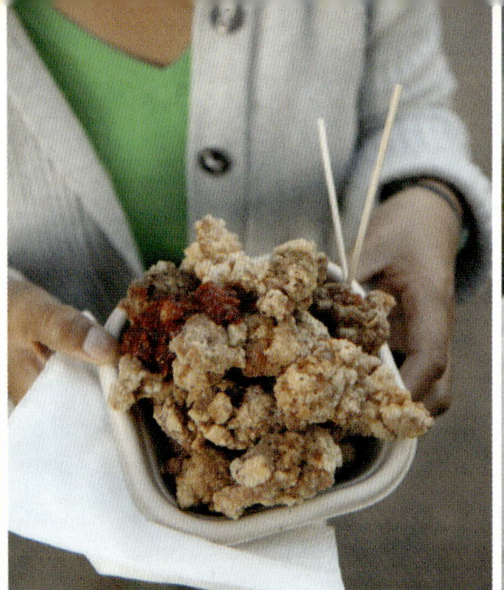

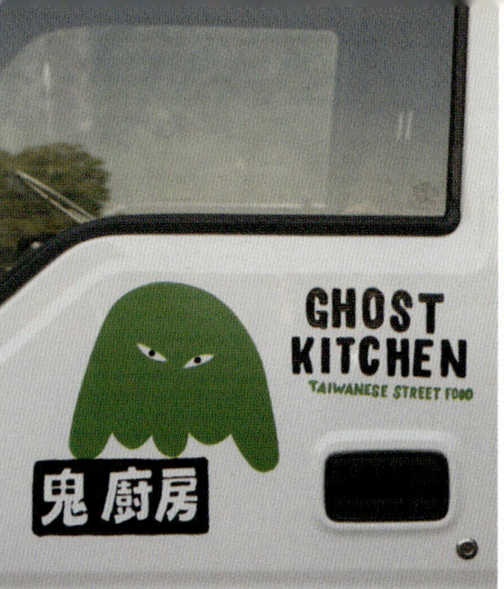

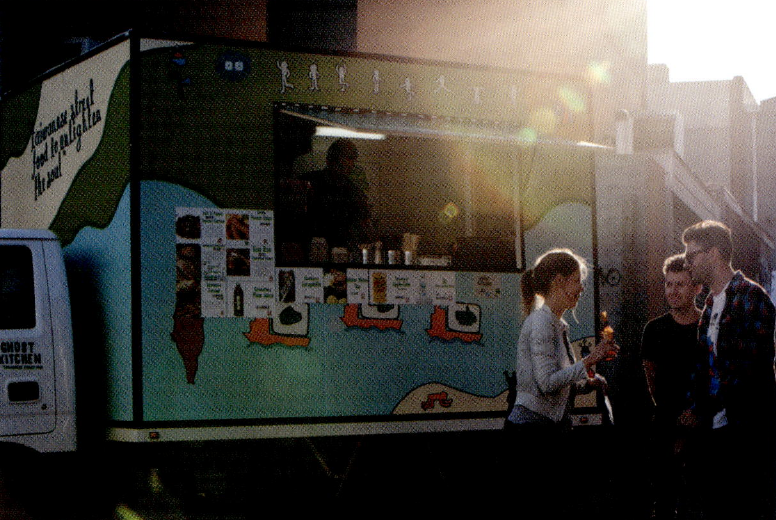

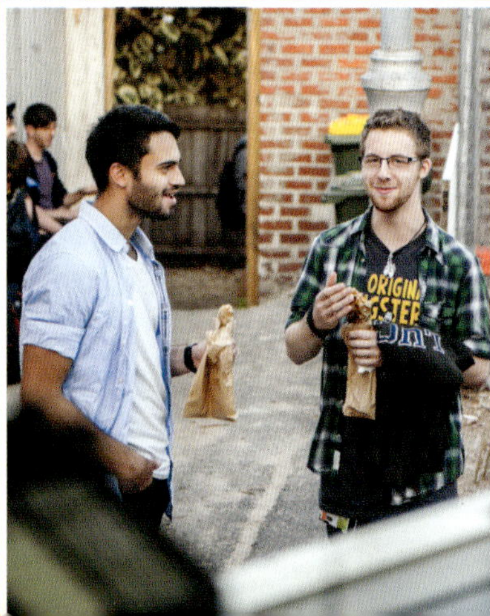

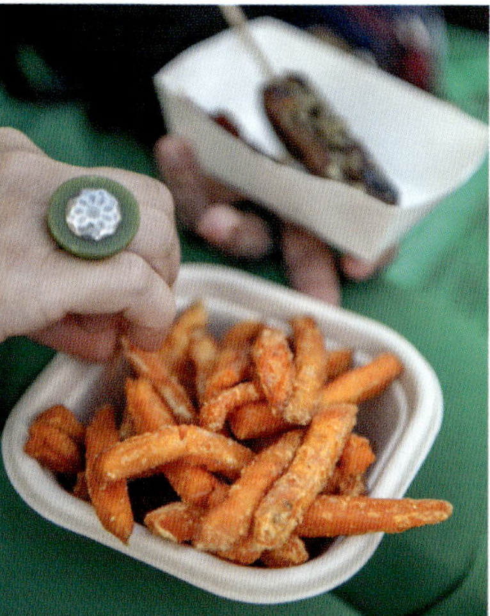

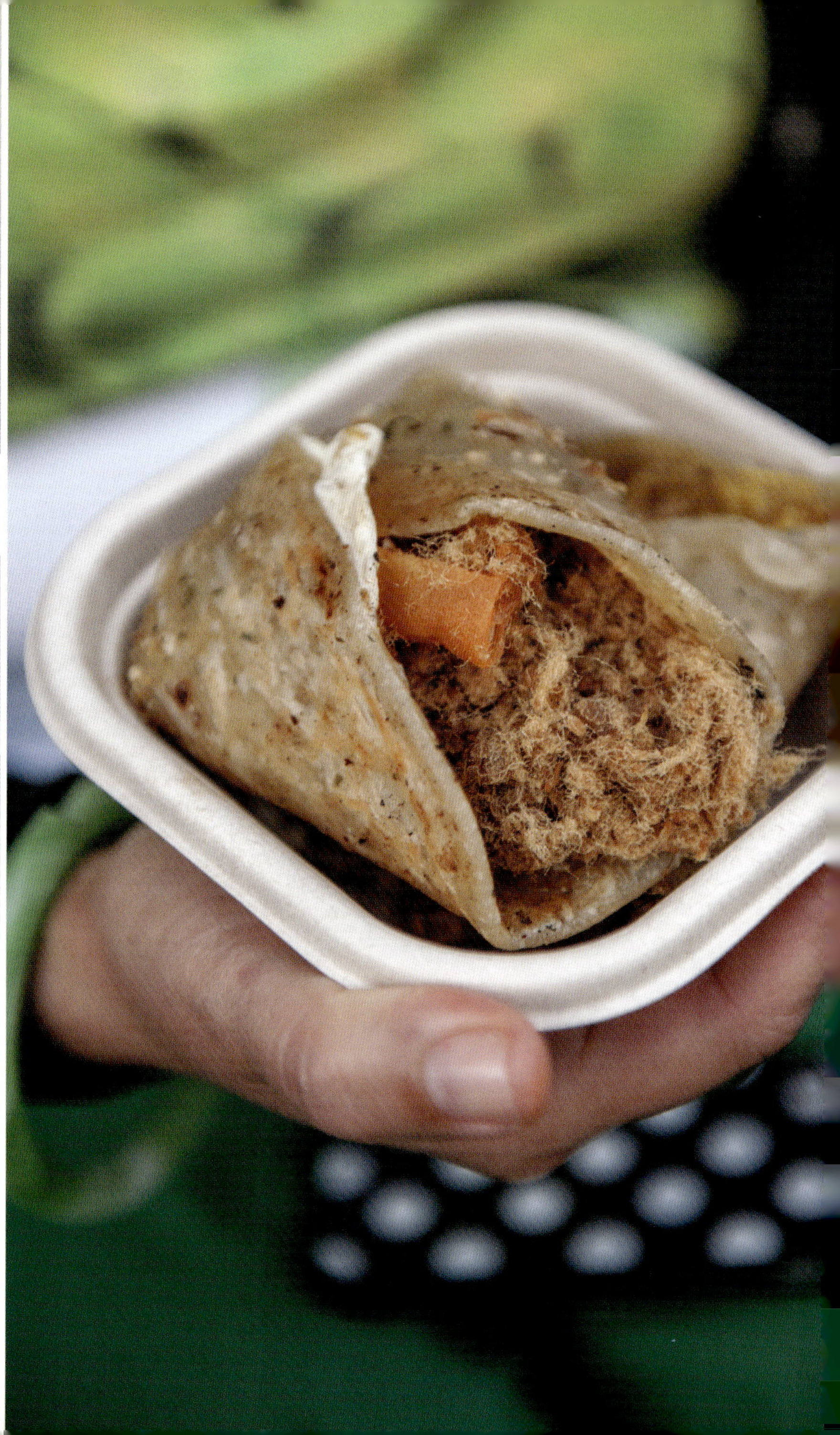

GHOST KITCHEN
鬼 廚房
GHOST KITCHEN
TAIWANESE STREET FOOD
GHOST KITCHEN
GHOST
KITCHEN
TAI

JUMPLINGS

Malaysian-born Roy arrived in Sydney, Australia in 1986 and worked as a web applications project manager for several years. A few years later, he and his family moved to Perth, seeking a quieter lifestyle.

The good folks in Perth should be grateful to Roy for then investing all of his energies into creating the best and most perfect dumpling. He went through several tonnes of flour and endless hours of experimentation, which has led to Jumpling's strong and loyal following. Roy acknowledges he has the least decorated truck on the streets, but it's just because he's been too busy focusing on perfecting his dumplings. The Jumplings Facebook page is also worth a look to get a sense of Roy's dumplings obsession, and his eccentric yet charming nature.

Roy is also passionate about the food truck scene in Perth, initiating the Perth Food Truck Rumble, as well as seminars for people interested in running their own food truck business. And it all seems to be paying off for Roy, as he's now opened up a couple of little bricks-and-mortar dumplings outlets in addition to his bus.

PORK JUMPLING

MAKES 30–35 DUMPLINGS

200 g pork mince (we suggest 85 per cent lean pork mince)

3 teaspoons soy sauce
1 teaspoon mirin
3 teaspoons oyster sauce
1 teaspoon sesame oil
1½ teaspoon sake (Japanese wine)
pinch of white pepper
2 teaspoons roasted bonito* stock
1 teaspoon sugar
½ teaspoon salt
⅛ cabbage, finely diced
⅛ wombok (Chinese cabbage), finely diced
1 spring onion, finely diced
¼ onion, finely diced
2 mm piece ginger, crushed
gyoza wrappers (note jumplings are bigger than regular dumplings)
2–3 tablespoons vegetable oil

DIPPING SAUCE
1 tablespoon lime
3 tablespoons soy sauce
pinch of caster sugar
1 tablespoon water, boiled and cooled

Place the pork into a large mixing bowl. Add the soy sauce, mirin, oyster sauce, sesame oil and sake, and mix thoroughly. Add the white pepper, stock, sugar and salt. Mix thoroughly and let sit for 10 minutes. Add the cabbage, wombok, spring onion, onion and ginger to the pork mixture. Cover with plastic wrap and leave to sit in the refrigerator for 30 minutes.

The salt will bring out the juices in the meat and vegetables. When you remove it from the refrigerator, mix it again before you start forming the dumplings to make sure the juices are all reabsorbed into the mixture.

Add a teaspoon full of filling to the wrapper. Using your fingers, fold the gyoza wrapper in half around the mixture, lining one side with water to help seal the edges. Place gyozas on a tray. Cover with plastic wrap and allow to sit in the refrigerator for 1 hour.

To make the dipping sauce, zest the lime carefully (do not add any of the white pith). Juice the lime, then add the lime zest and juice to the soy sauce and sugar and balance with cooled boiled water. The lime should enhance the flavour of the soy sauce. The dipping sauce should taste salty and fruity with only a little sweetness.

Remove the dumplings from the refrigerator. Heat the vegetable oil in a large non-stick frying pan. Once the oil is hot, add the chilled dumplings (or jumplings) one by one. Add 125 ml (½ cup) of water to the pan (or enough to half cover the dumplings in the pan) and cover with the lid. Cook on medium–high heat for 5–6 minutes. The water will evaporate during this time and the bottom of the jumplings will brown slightly. Remove from the pan.

Serve the jumplings hot, on a bed of cabbage with the dipping sauce on the side. One person should be able to eat all of this … so make some more!

** Bonito is a type of tuna. Bonito stock is similar to chicken stock. It forms the basis for most Japanese cooking and can be purchased from Japanese stores. You can use chicken stock as an alternative.*

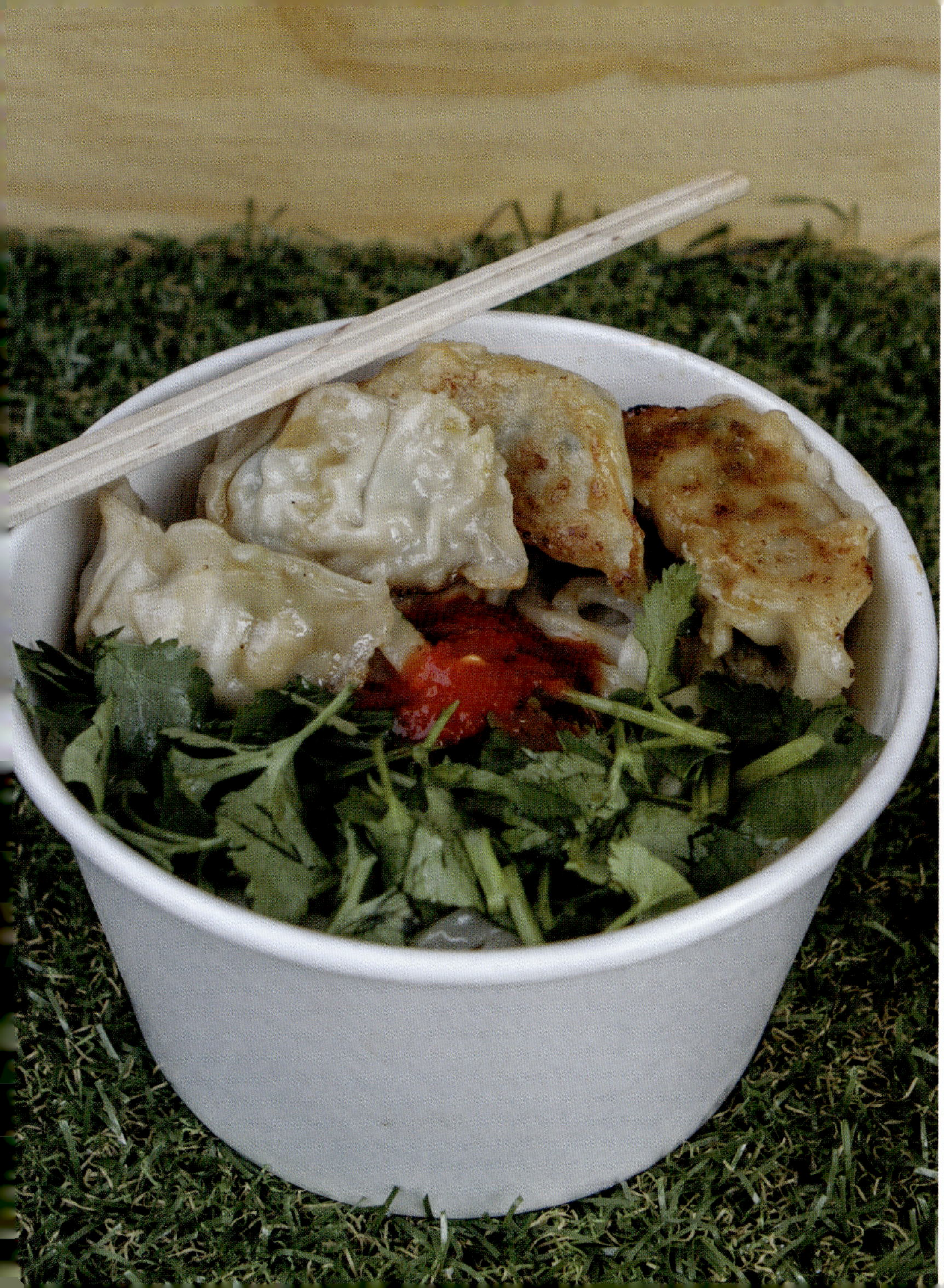

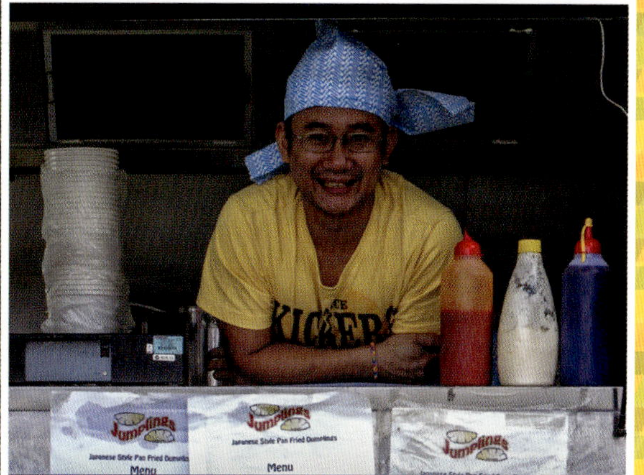

Jumplings
Tasty dumplings

LIL' NOM NOMS

Lil' Nom Noms owner NamDo remembers very little about coming to Australia with his family as a refugee at the age of two. But he does recall that the refugee life wasn't an easy one; he had few toys to play with, clothes that never quite fit, and had to work as a teenager to help his parents with basic expenses. Like many immigrants, NamDo also grew up with a desire to fit in, which explains why he preferred pizzas over steamed pork buns as a child. Fortunately for NamDo, as he grew up he came to his senses, and found a way to reconcile the Vietnamese and Australian cultures he's intrinsically bound to.

After 20-odd years with numerous jobs in hospitality management in London and Australia, NamDo took a job in event management, in search of a seemingly better and more financially stable lifestyle. He confesses that during this time 'the money was awesome and the parties even better', but ultimately he realised the corporate world couldn't give him the 'mental reward' that he still yearned for. So with his heart still in the food industry, he returned to his Vietnamese roots, finding it more viable to start up a one-man food truck than committing to a bricks-and-mortar eatery.

Lil' Nom Noms sells Vietnamese street food favourites like bánh mì baguettes, vermicelli salads, steamed bao burgers filled with pork belly and coleslaw, and even a Vietnamese take on tacos. Despite often having to work in extreme weather conditions (it can be 40ºC or hotter in the van on a summer day), NamDo values the personal exchanges he has with his customers.

RICE NOODLE SALAD WITH GRILLED LEMONGRASS CHICKEN

- -

SERVES 4

LEMONGRASS PASTE

2 stalks lemongrass, finely chopped
2 spring onions, finely chopped
4 garlic cloves, finely chopped
80 ml (⅓ cup) fish sauce

450 g chicken thighs, cut into bite-size pieces
2 small red chillies, finely chopped
55 g (¼ cup) white sugar
70 ml lime or lemon juice
60 ml (¼ cup) rice vinegar
250 g fresh rice vermicelli noodles
¼ wombok (Chinese cabbage), thinly sliced
2 Lebanese cucumbers, julienned
1 carrot, julienned
90 g (1 cup) bean sprouts
45 g (1½ cups) coriander leaves, loosely packed
15 g (1½ cups) Vietnamese mint leaves, loosely packed

roasted peanuts or fried shallots, coarsely chopped, to serve

To prepare the lemongrass paste, combine lemongrass, spring onions and 3 garlic cloves in a food processor or mortar and pestle, and process or grind to a coarse paste. Add 15 ml (1 tablespoon) fish sauce, season to taste with sea salt and freshly ground black pepper and grind to combine.

Place the chicken thighs and lemongrass paste in a non-reactive medium-size bowl (i.e. glass, ceramic or stainless steel, *not* aluminium), toss to coat the chicken. Cover with plastic wrap and leave in the refrigerator to marinate for 1 hour.

Prepare the dressing in a medium-size bowl. Combine the remaining garlic clove and fish sauce, chillies, sugar, lime or lemon juice and rice vinegar, and stir until the sugar dissolves. Set dressing aside.

Place the rice vermicelli noodles in a heat-proof bowl, cover with boiling water and stir, using chopsticks to separate the noodles. Drain and refresh in cold water, then drain again.

Heat a chargrill pan over medium heat. Remove the chicken from the refrigerator, and grill until lightly browned and cooked through. Remove from the pan and slice thinly.

Combine the noodles, wombok, cucumber, carrot, bean sprouts and coriander and mint leaves in a large bowl. Add sliced chicken to the noodle salad, drizzle with dressing and toss to combine. Divide salad among bowls, scatter with roasted peanuts or fried shallots and serve immediately.

TUK TUK TUCKSHOP: *Asian adventures*

LIL'
NOM
NOM'
w: www.lilnomnoms.com.au
Vietnamese inspired street food

TUK TUK TUCKSHOP: Asian adventures

NEM N' NEM

Ken and Kathy, the brother-and-sister team behind Nem n' Nem, originally came to Australia from northern Vietnam to study as a chef and mortgage broker respectively. Ken found work as a chef in Launceston, Tasmania, but soon found himself wanting to run his own kitchen. So together with Kathy, they decided to try their hand at running a food truck business.

Growing up in Hanoi, Ken and Kathy were familiar with street food and the strong cultural tradition of preparing meals with their family while sharing stories. From the age of ten children sat with the adults to help make nem rolls – rice-paper rolls filled with a variety of ingredients and fried.

The menu is quite varied and changes every so often, but includes such staples as the Nem n' Nem rolls, pho soups, vermicelli noodle salads, bánh mì rolls and nem nuong (char-grilled pork sausage skewers).

SEAFOOD NEM FRIED ROLL

MAKES UP TO 25 ROLLS

250 g fresh prawns, peeled
250 g calamari
250 g (3⅓ cups) brown onion, finely diced
250 g (4 cups) celery, grated
2 teaspoons brown sugar
1 teaspoon salt
1 teaspoon fine white pepper
3 tablespoons mayonnaise
15 spring roll wrappers, 2.5 cm (8½ inch) squares
cornflour
1 tablespoon rice flour
175 g (1¾ cups) fresh breadcrumbs
vegetable oil

SWEET CHILLI MAYONNAISE DIPPING SAUCE

1½ tablespoons sweet chilli sauce
4 tablespoons mayonnaise

Half fill a large saucepan with water and bring to the boil. Drop in the prawns and calamari and cook for 30 seconds. Remove from the heat, drain and cool under cold running water.

Cut prawns and calamari into small cubes and put them into a large bowl with the onion, celery, sugar, salt, pepper and mayonnaise. Mix.

Cut the spring roll wrappers diagonally to form two triangles, and then separate them into single sheets.

Place a piece of wrapper on a plate with the base of the triangle facing you. Spoon about 1 tablespoon of the mixture onto the middle of the bottom edge of the wrapper and fold the two adjacent sides into the centre, one on top of the other.

Roll the base of the wrapper toward the apex to form a nice firm roll, and secure with a dab of cornflour mixed with some water. Repeat until you have filled all of the wrappers.

In a small saucepan, over medium heat, mix the rice flour with some cold water to make a thick, clear liquid. Set it aside to cool down.

Spread the breadcrumbs on a small flat tray. One by one, dip the rolls into the rice-flour liquid, then roll them through the breadcrumbs. Repeat until you have covered all nem rolls with breadcrumbs.

The nem rolls are best cooked in a deep-fryer in vegetable oil heated to 170ºC. Alternatively, cook the rolls in a large saucepan or deep frying pan. You can also store them in the freezer and cook when needed. If cooking from frozen, just carefully slide frozen nem rolls in the hot oil (do not defrost) and cook for an additional minute or so.

To make the sweet chilli mayonnaise dipping sauce simply mix both ingredients together and serve straight away.

Nem N' Nem
VIETNAMESE HAWKER KITCHEN

pho
bo
gai

NUOC MAMA'S FOOD TRUCK

BÁNH XÈO
SAVOURY CRISPY PANCAKE

- -

This pancake is gluten free and can be easily customised to your personal tastes, from an aromatic lemongrass chicken filling to a more delicate seafood smorgasbord.

SERVES 8

PANCAKE MIXTURE
500 g rice flour
3 tablespoons ground turmeric
½ teaspoon salt
1 bunch spring onions
2 medium white onions, sliced
1 tin (400 ml) coconut milk
125 ml (½ cup) water

NUOC MAM CHAM
125 ml (½ cup) warm water
200 g sugar
250 ml (1 cup) fish sauce
3 tablespoons vinegar
½ lemon, juiced
2 garlic cloves, crushed
1 chilli, finely chopped

FILLING
prawn, pork or whatever tickles your fancy
1 garlic clove, crushed
1 teaspoon fish sauce
500 g beanshoots

To make the pancake mixture combine the dry ingredients first in a large bowl, then add the coconut milk. Whisk together well.

The consistency is essential for a crispy and light pancake. Slowly add the water until the consistency resembles a thin, smooth stream of liquid. Once the desired consistency is achieved, place uncovered in the refrigerator and leave the mixture to set for at least 5–10 minutes. *Note: The pancake mixture needs time to sit to allow the turmeric and coconut milk and rice flour to fully combine. This mixture will keep in the refrigerator for no more than 1 day.*

Next, prepare the nuoc mam cham dipping sauce by putting the sugar and warm water in a small bowl. Stir until the sugar is dissolved. Then add the fish sauce vinegar and lemon juice and adjust the taste to your liking before finishing the sauce by adding the garlic and chilli.

To prepare the filling take your choice of prawn and/or pork and stir-fry along with some garlic, onions and a dash fish sauce. Slightly undercook the filling ingredients as they will be cooked again in the crispy pancake. Set the filling aside until you are ready to make your pancakes.

Tip: Bánh Xèo is a versatile dish, so if prawn or pork is not your thing, then they can easily be substituted with chicken, fish, tofu or thinly sliced vegetables.

Now for the fun part! In a large frying pan (the larger the better) heat some vegetable oil over medium heat and lightly fry a handful of spring and white onions. Then slowly pour a full ladle of the pancake mixture into the centre of the pan and swirl the pan until the bottom and sides of the pan are covered with the mixture. Allow the mixture to cook a little, then add some of the filling to one half of the pan and cover with a handful of bean sprouts. Cover the frying pan with a lid and cook for 2–3 minutes. The pancake will sizzle away. The lid is ready to come off when the entire pancake mixture is cooked and the sides of the pancake have begun to brown. You can peek to check.

Grab an egg flip or spatula, and turn the empty side of the pancake over to cover the filling, like an omelette. Allow the bottom to crisp for another minute or two and then it is ready to eat.

The pancake is best served with fresh lettuce, Vietnamese mint, perilla leaf (available from most Asian supermarkets) and other fresh herbs. And don't forget to dip the pancake in the nuoc mam cham sauce! It brings the various elements of the pancake and fresh greens together in a giant party of flavours in your mouth.

An Ngon (Eat well; enjoy)!

For young Vietnamese couple Linda and Andrew, Nuoc Mama's Food Truck is their first ever business venture. Each of them studied in non-food related fields; Linda studied commerce and marketing, while Andrew dabbled in law and graphic design. But it was Linda's family restaurant that ultimately inspired them to start up a food truck business together.

Growing up in a tight-knit Vietnamese community, the pair undertook a rigorous process to develop and refine their menu, seeking approval from the toughest of critics – their parents and grandparents, for whom food is a vital part of their culture. The name of the truck is also a cheeky adaptation of the 'mother' of all Vietnamese ingredients, nuoc mam or fish sauce, which is used either as a base or an addition to many Vietnamese dishes.

Nuoc Mama's menu changes regularly but includes rice-paper rolls, bánh mì baguettes, pho soups and their signature bánh xèo, a crispy pancake that takes its name from the sizzling sound it makes when the batter is swirled into a hot pan. The dish is a versatile base for a range of fillings, which in Nuoc Mama's case may include a prawn or pork filling with fresh lettuce, mint, perilla leaves and other fresh herbs. This mama (and papa) sure do keep their so-called Nuoc children well fed!

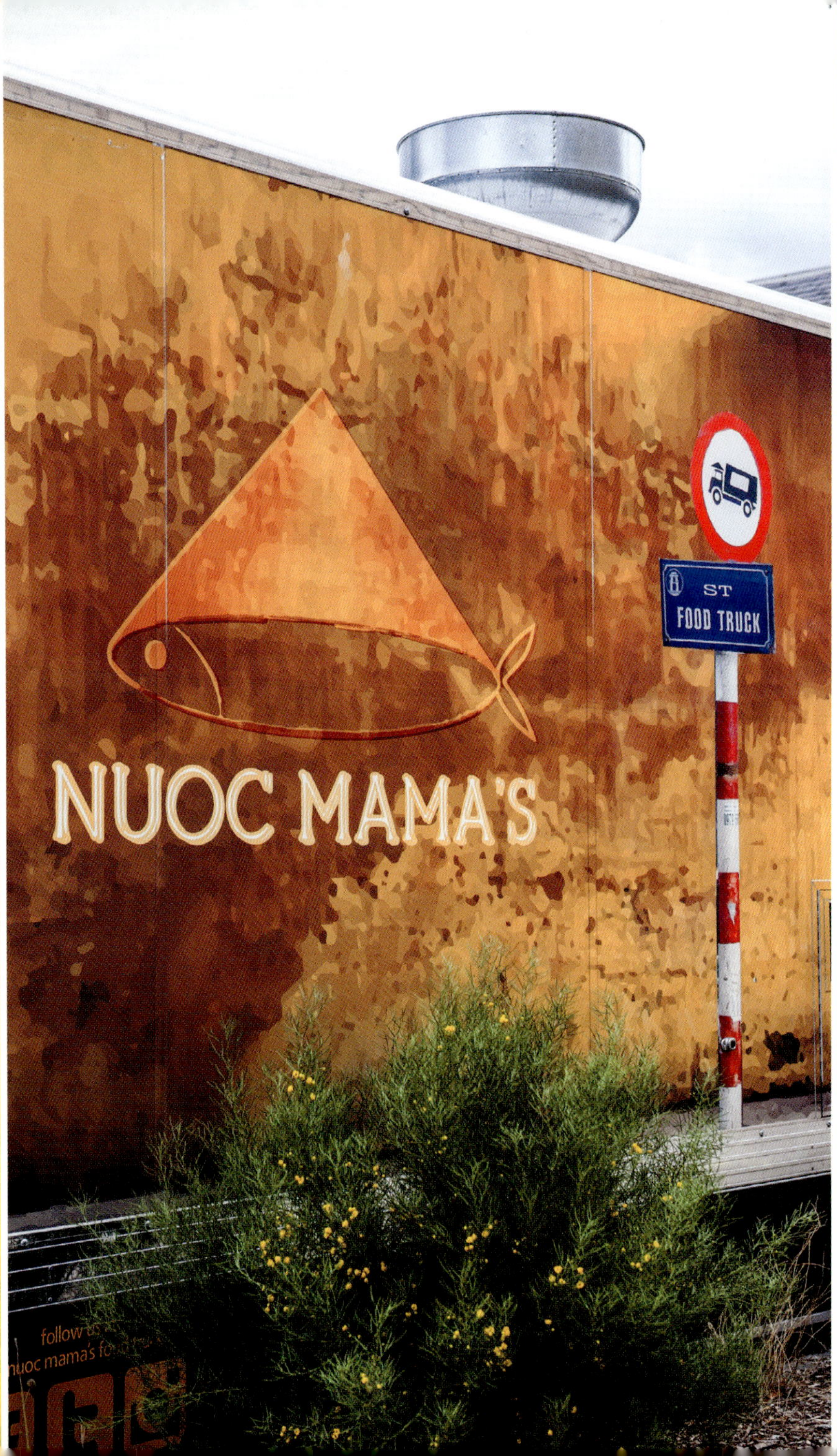
NUOC MAMA'S
ST
FOOD TRUCK

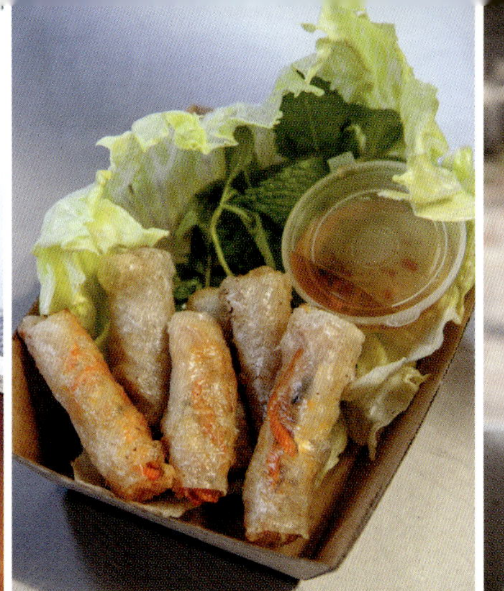

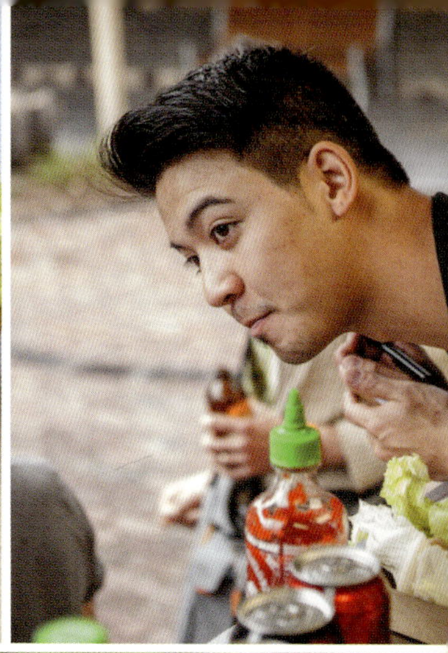

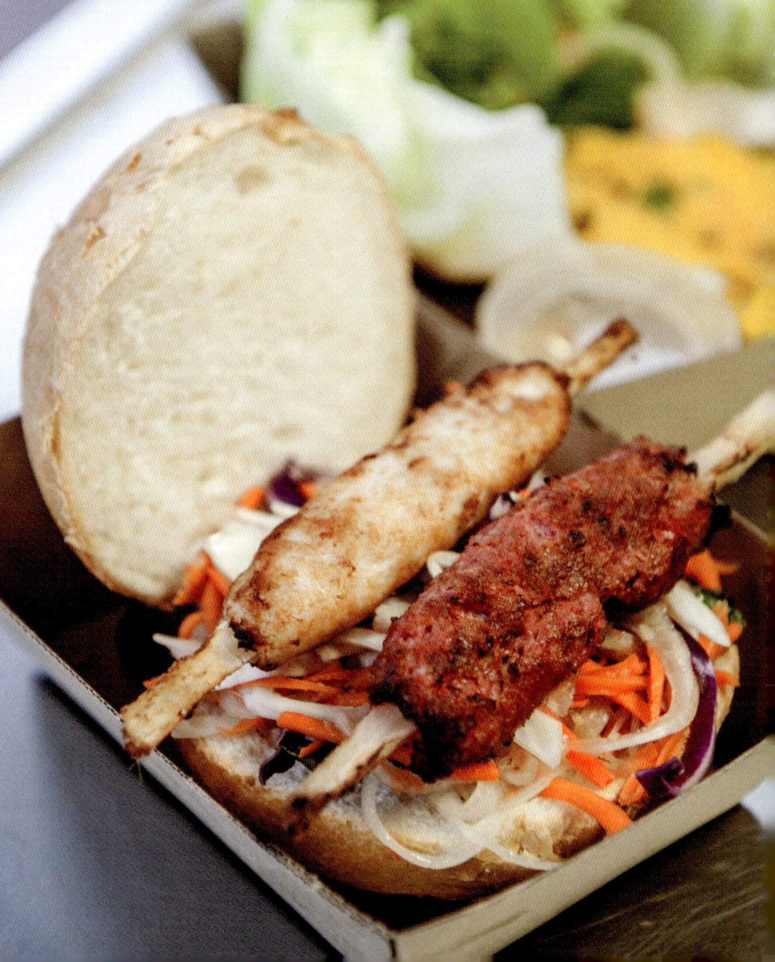

OOODLE LISHIOUS

Ooodle Lishious food truck owner Mel left Vietnam with her family in the 1970s in an illegal vessel, headed towards an unknown but hopefully brighter future. After three days in a leaky boat they were rescued by an illegal Japanese whaling ship.

Then aged three, Mel's parents kept her quiet during the journey with the promise that she would one day attend a beautiful wedding in a new country. Just the idea of such a future was magical to Mel. The family was processed in Japan before migrating to New Zealand, where they lived for ten years. Seeking a larger Vietnamese community they moved to Australia in 1994 and now regard Melbourne as home.

Mel first learned to cook at a very young age, helping her mother, who had left Vietnam without knowing how to cook. Over the years Vietnamese cooking, especially from the southern region, grew into a genuine interest for Mel. Now with her husband Matt they bring authentic vermicelli noodle salads, rice-paper rolls and pho soups to Melbourne locals.

SOUTHERN VIETNAM'S BROTHY PINEAPPLE SOUP

Canh thơm

Fruit is frequently used to create savoury soups in (southern) Vietnamese cooking. Pineapples are used in a broth soup called canh chua thơm *(sour soup with pineapples and other vegetables). It is similar to a Thai tom yum, but* canh chua thơm *has a cleaner and sharper taste. Prawns or fish are the most often used proteins.*

The OoOdle Lishious variation is simplified, substituting prawns with tofu, making it vegetarian and vegan!

SERVES 4–5

2 Asian pineapples*
2 tablespoons oil (canola or vegetable oil)
750 ml–1 litre (3–4 cups) water
200 g cubed tofu (fresh or pre-fried)
rice paddy herbs, chopped*

To prepare the pineapples, cut off the green spiky top, and remove the skin from the sides; cut as close to the edge of the pineapple skin as possible, leaving exposed a bunch of brown scraggly dots, called eyes. Remove these 'eyes' separately by cutting into the pineapple with a small knife, forming V-shaped trenches as you move around the pineapple. Using a small knife loosely 'shave' the pineapple into pieces until you reach the core.

In a large pot, heat canola or vegetable oil over medium heat and sauté the pineapple pieces. Toss the pineapple pieces so that they don't burn, and allow the juice to come out. Depending on the seasonal sweetness or tartness of the pineapple, add sugar to taste. We usually add about 2 tablespoons. Continue to sauté the pineapples, until the sugar is dissolved and pineapples are somewhat softened. Add the water to the pot; this will become the broth.

Add a pinch of salt or splash of fish sauce to bring out the pineapple flavour. Add the tofu and bring to the boil. Simmer for about 2 minutes. Remove from heat and generously add rice paddy herbs. Rice paddy herbs are best added to the broth just before serving so that they retain their crispness.

Serve with white rice or rice vermicelli noodles.

**Asian pineapples are available from most Asian supermarkets. They are generally smaller and sweeter than western pineapples. You can use western pineapples instead of Asian pineapples, just adjust the sugar accordingly to suit your taste.*

**Rice paddy herbs are available from Asian supermarkets.*

OoOdleLishious
Vietnamese Street Kitchen
STREET TRADING * PRIVATE FUNCTIONS * MARKETS & EVENTS

OoOdleLishious

PHAT BUDDHA ROLLS

Sokha and Joel were high school sweethearts, but broke up to pursue other experiences and other relationships. A few years down the track, fate – or, in fact, Facebook – brought the two back together again.

Sokha is of Cambodian heritage and came to Australia at the age of two. Being the eldest of five children, she learnt to cook at an early age. In Cambodian culture recipes are rarely written down and taught simply by cooking together as a family.

Joel who is part German and part Lebanese also shares an interest in food, so when their romance was rekindled, they decided to also take their love of food to the streets.

With a decked-out vintage caravan that has been spray-painted by local street-art collective Cold Krush, Phat Buddha Rolls serves Cambodian bread rolls filled with delicious marinated meats, vermicelli salads and rice-paper rolls.

CHAR KREUNG

Spicy lemongrass, chicken and green capsicum stir-fry

SERVES 6–8

KREUNG (LEMONGRASS PASTE)

4 lemongrass stalks
30 g (½ cup) kaffir lime leaves
50 g (½ cup) fresh turmeric
1 garlic bulb
50 g (¼ cup) galangal, finely grated
3–5 hot chillies (depending on personal preference)

4 tablespoons vegetable or olive oil
125 g (½ cup) kreung
2 tablespoons pickled mud fish paste*
1 kg chicken, mince
1 tablespoon fish sauce
2 tablespoons palm sugar (or raw sugar)
1 teaspoon white vinegar
2 green capsicums, chopped into 2 cm × 2 cm squares
1 brown onion, chopped into 2 cm × 2 cm squares

30 g (1 cup) of fresh holy basil, to garnish

To make the kreung place all ingredients in the bowl of a food processor, and add water until the bowl is half full. Blend to form a paste with a fine consistency.

Heat the oil in a wok. Add the kreung and mud fish pastes (watch out for bones in the mud fish paste, remove them if you find any). Stir until the pastes combine and the liquid has reduced by half.

Add the chicken mince and stir until the chicken juice has reduced. Add the fish sauce, palm sugar and vinegar, and stir for 4 minutes. Add the capsicum and stir for another 2 minutes, then add the onion and turn the heat off.

Stir holy basil through the stir-fry and serve with steamed rice.

** Pickled mud fish paste is available from most Asian supermarkets.*

PHAT BUDDHA ROLLS

070

CAMBODIAN ROLLS!
PHAT BUDDHA ROLLS
LIKE US ON FACEBOOK

PHAT BUDDHA ROLLS
PHAT BUDDHA ROLLS

PHAT BUDDHA ROLLS

THE SATAY HUT

CHICKEN LARB WITH THAI PICKLE

SERVES 4

THAI PICKLE
115 g (½ cup) white sugar
125 ml (½ cup) white vinegar
1 tablespoon coarse cooking salt
125 ml (½ cup) water
1 red capsicum, sliced
45 g (½ cup) bean sprouts
1 Lebanese cucumber, sliced

60 ml (¼ cup) chicken stock
2 tablespoons lime juice
1 tablespoon fish sauce
1 tablespoon palm sugar, grated (or brown sugar)
500 g chicken mince
1 garlic clove, crushed
2 spring onions, sliced
1 tablespoon fresh mint, chopped
1 fresh long chilli, chopped

1 medium iceberg lettuce, shredded

First, make the Thai pickle. In a medium-size saucepan, bring the sugar, vinegar, salt and water to the boil. Allow mixture to cool. Once cool, place remaining ingredients in a bowl and pour this mixture over them. Let stand for half an hour.

In a large frying pan or saucepan bring the stock, lime juice, fish sauce and sugar to the boil. Add the chicken mince and garlic, and lower the heat to a simmer, stir until cooked through. Allow to cool, then stir in the spring onions, mint and chilli. Serve on a bed of shredded lettuce with the Thai pickle on the side.

The Satay Hut owner Adam decided the year he turned 40 would be the year he gave up his long-time career in scaffolding, and committed to a more fulfilling and family-friendly career. So it was in 2013 that he took to the roads with the intention of selling his satays and other Asian-inspired dishes.

Like many, Adam tested out his food truck business at markets, first from a marquee and then from a second-hand trailer. Some might say he was given a divine pat on the back for the choice he made, because the second-hand trailer he sought to buy was conveniently called the Satay Hut. Perfect for his new business!

But the inspiration to join the growing fleet of food trucks in Adelaide, Australia only came after going with his family to WOMAD, a massive global music festival. Held every year in the Adelaide Botanic Gardens, it is also a vibrant smorgasbord of international foods.

TUK TUK TUCKSHOP: *Asian adventures*

TSURU

Tsuru was one of ten food trucks accepted into the one-year Sydney Food Truck Trial. Unlike other cities in Australia, where the food truck scene grew a little more organically, the City of Sydney put hundreds of contenders through a long and gruelling application process. After this, the final contenders were pitted against each other in a MasterChef-style cook-off, which was judged by local food experts and critics. Tsuru's winning place reinforces the fact that it's possible to get restaurant-quality food on the streets, served out of a truck.

Truck owner Ellyn started Tsuru after working in marketing for a few years. Born in Surabaya, Indonesia, Ellyn originally came to Sydney,

Australia to study commerce, but eventually returned to the thing she loved most – cooking. For Asian families cooking is a task shared among its members and passed on from generation to generation; coming from a family of restaurateurs was an added benefit for Ellyn.

Tsuru's menu features authentic Asian street food including steamed buns that are proudly made in-house using recipes passed on from Ellyn's family. These steamed 'burger' buns are then filled with Ellyn's signature pork belly, beef and kimchi or lamb rendang. There are also bread rolls filled with lemongrass chicken or pork, and a selection of rice-paper rolls. For dessert you can treat yourself with a slice of the vivid-green pandan cake.

CHICKEN SATAY STICKS

SERVES 4

1 Lebanese cucumber, finely chopped
1 carrot, finely chopped
1 Asian eschalot*, finely chopped
1 tablespoon rice vinegar
1½ tablespoons caster sugar
½ teaspoon salt
40 g unsalted butter, melted
80 ml (⅓ cup) kecap manis
2 garlic cloves
300 g skinless chicken thigh fillets, cut into 1.5 cm cubes

PEANUT SAUCE

110 g (¾ cup) salted roasted peanuts
3 macadamia nuts
1 long red chilli, seeded, roughly chopped
1 onion, chopped
1 tablespoon coconut sugar*
¼ teaspoon shrimp paste*
2 tablespoons sunflower oil

Begin this recipe a day ahead.

In an airtight container mix together the cucumber, carrot, eschalot, rice vinegar, caster sugar and salt, and refrigerate overnight.

Soak 8 wooden skewers in warm water for 20 minutes.

Mix melted butter, 40 ml (2 tablespoons) of the kecap manis and 1 garlic clove, finely chopped, in a medium bowl. Add the chicken to the marinade, and coat evenly. Cover and set aside.

To make the peanut sauce, place the peanuts, macadamias, chilli, remaining garlic clove, onion, coconut sugar and shrimp paste in a food processor and blend to form a paste.

Heat the oil in a non-stick fry pan over low–medium heat and add the paste. Cook, stirring constantly, for 4 minutes, or until the mixture starts to become slightly dry. Add 200 ml water and the remaining 40 ml (2 tablespoons) of kecap manis, and stir to combine. Bring to the boil, then simmer, stirring constantly, for 5–10 minutes, or until the sauce starts to look glossy. Season to taste.

Set aside 60 ml (¼ cup) of the peanut sauce. Stir 100 ml water into remaining peanut sauce to thin it slightly and transfer it to a serving bowl.

Heat a chargrill pan or barbecue. Thread the chicken onto skewers. Coat skewers generously with the reserved peanut sauce and cook, turning constantly, for 6–8 minutes, until browned and cooked through. Serve with peanut sauce and cucumber pickles. Any remaining peanut sauce can be stored in an airtight container in the fridge for 2–3 days.

**Asian eschalots, coconut sugar and shrimp paste are available from most Asian supermarkets.*

tsuru
PORK BELLY BUN
BEEF KIMCHI
PORK BUN
CHILLI TOFU RICE
BEEF KIMCHI RICE
PORK BELLY RICE
/TSURUFOODTRUCK
TSURU.COM.AU

/TSURUFOODTRUCK

WHITE GUY COOKS THAI

This white guy certainly can cook Thai, but truth be told, he can actually cook up quite a range of things. Having clocked up 15-odd years in the hospitality industry, owner Simon was first introduced to Thai cuisine by another chef. He had, until then, worked mainly in French fine-dining cuisine, and admits that following this he went a little 'Thai-food crazy' for a few years. Since then he has travelled around Asia, where he regularly seeks out local cooking classes to build his Asian cooking skills.

White Guy Cooks Thai is one of the 'older' trucks in Melbourne, Australia. In an industry that is still young and growing, Simon is a well-known figure, ever willing to offer advice and share his experiences with fellow truck compadres. Building on his success, look out for Simon's latest food truck addition, Korean Fried Chicken, on the road.

12-HOUR SLOW-ROASTED PORK BELLY

Visit your local Vietnamese butcher and ask for the thickest cut of boneless belly – the cut with only a few chine bones (small connective bones) if any. There is one cut like this on each side of the pig and it is the only one you want to use for this recipe.

If you use the belly cuts from around the ribs, once the fat melts you will have little remaining for your bánh mì!

SERVES 12

230 g (1 cup) caster sugar
130 g (1 cup) sea salt
1.5 kg pork belly
400 g duck fat (pork back fat works well too)

Combine the sugar and salt in a bowl. Place the pork belly in a large roasting tray, and then rub the sugar and salt mixture into the pork belly. Then allow it to cure on a bench, covered with plastic wrap or a tea towel, for at least 12 hours, but not more than 24 hours.

Wash off the salt and sugar and place the pork belly snugly in a pan with duck fat packed in up to the level of the skin. Dry the skin with a paper towel and slow roast in a fan-forced oven at the lowest temperature for at least 12 hours, but not more than 18 hours (8 hours or more is okay if in a hurry).

Once the desired time is reached, crank the oven to its highest temperature to get the crackling nice and sexy. Check the pork belly after 15 minutes to keep a close eye on it because it can burn quite quickly.

When the crackling is to your liking, remove the pork belly from the oven and check for bones (the meat will have pulled away to expose them). Remove them carefully with tongs and twist as you pull them out so as not to tear the meat.

Place the pork belly in the fridge with a tray or chopping board on top and a few cans of beans or similar to weigh it down. Leave it for 8 hours or so. When cold, place the pork belly crackling side down and carefully slice it into 6–8 mm slices.

In a hot pan heat a little duck fat and fry slices a few minutes on each side before serving in a fresh Vietnamese bánh mì roll with Kewpie (Japanese) mayonnaise, Asian coleslaw, tomato jam, chilli and coriander. Enjoy!

TUK TUK TUCKSHOP: *Asian adventures*

WHITE GUY
COOKS THAI!

CHEEKY AUSSIE BITES

AGAPÉ ORGANIC FOOD TRUCK

Mind the accent on top of the 'e' in the name Agapé. The word has several meanings, but among the various interpretations is a feast shared as a sign of love and friendship. With a truck name derived from Greek, a chef whose mother is a Chinese-born Indonesian and whose father has English and Scandinavian heritage, and a menu that's partially American-inspired but regularly changing, the Agapé Organic Food Truck stubbornly defies categorisation.

Owner Simon has close to twenty years experience in the food industry. And in contrast to many new truck owners, Simon also runs a successful bricks-and-mortar restaurant in Botany, Sydney. Having both businesses means resources, including kitchens, staff and ingredients, can be shared. This is especially useful as Simon follows a nose-to-tail philosophy, purchasing whole organic pigs and lambs, and aiming to use as much as possible with minimal wastage.

Yet one thing that differs from his restaurant is that Simon's 'truck food' is decidedly 'street food'. There's plenty of love to feast on, such as pulled pork or beef rolls, organic spelt hotdogs, chilli fries and chilli con o sin (with or without) carne. For dessert, the dish that will leave your mouth 'agape' in utter wonder is the chocolate spelt brownie with a nut praline over the top. Awesome.

14-HOUR SLOW-COOKED PULLED PORK ON A SPELT BUN WITH HOMEMADE BARBECUE SAUCE, COLESLAW AND SALSA VERDE

MAKES 12 BUNS

12 spelt (or other) buns

PULLED PORK

1 whole pork shoulder, bone in
1 teaspoon chilli powder
1 tablespoon ground cumin
1 tablespoon ground coriander
1 tablespoon smoked paprika
1 tablespoon sweet paprika
1 tablespoon ground cinnamon
1 tablespoon ground ginger
1 tablespoon ground white pepper
3 tablespoons raw sugar
1 tablespoon salt

HOMEMADE BARBECUE SAUCE

120 ml rice bran oil
2 brown onions, sliced
1 garlic clove, chopped
1 tin or 500 g (2½ cups) tomatoes, chopped
1 tablespoon smoked paprika
1 tablespoon sweet paprika
4 tablespoons raw sugar
1 tablespoon salt
50 ml balsamic vinegar

COLESLAW

½ small cabbage, cored and thinly sliced
aioli or mayonnaise

SALSA VERDE

2 bunches flat-leaf parsley
1 garlic clove
120 ml rice bran oil

To make the pork, make incisions all over the pork shoulder with a small knife. Combine all spices in a large bowl, then place the pork shoulder inside and rub to coat evenly and thoroughly with spices. Cover with plastic wrap and leave to marinate overnight in the refrigerator.

Set your oven to the lowest temperature possible and place the pork on a baking tray. Pour a cup of water into the baking tray to prevent it from drying out. *Note: if the pork shoulder has had the skin removed you will need to first cover it with greaseproof paper and then with foil before adding the water. This will protect the pork whilst cooking.*

Bake in the oven for around 14 hours, or until soft to touch. Once cooked allow to cool just enough so you can get your hands into the pork and start pulling the meat off the bone.

To make the barbecue sauce heat the rice bran oil in a medium-size pot and add the onions. Cook the onions until they're dark golden brown. Add the remaining ingredients and cook for 30 minutes. Allow to cool slightly, then blend in a food processor.

To make the coleslaw add just enough aioli to dress the cabbage. Season with a pinch of salt.

To make the salsa verde put all the ingredients in a blender, and blend together until combined, adding a touch more oil if needed to make it thick and smooth.

To construct, cut into the bun lengthways (but only half-way through so that it remains intact). Lay the bun open in the oven and toast for a couple of minutes. Once toasted add the coleslaw and pulled pork to the bun, then spoon over the homemade barbecue sauce, and finally the salsa verde. Enjoy!

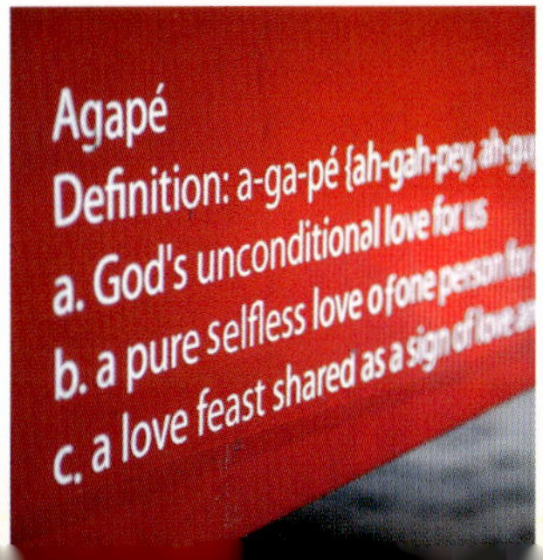

Agapé
Definition: a-ga-pé {ah-gah-pey, ah-gah
a. God's unconditional love for us
b. a pure selfless love of one person for
c. a love feast shared as a sign of love a

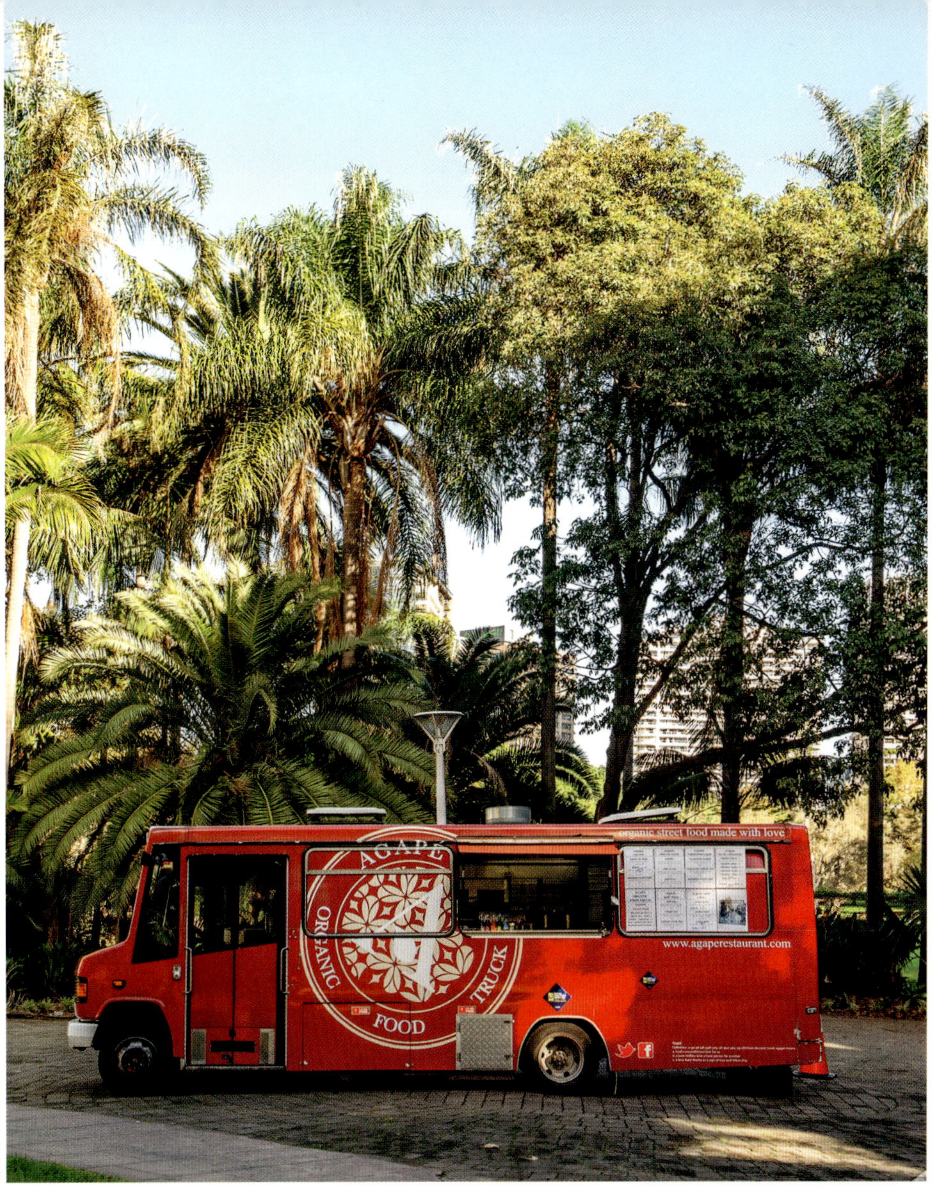

DIGGING FOR FIRE BBQ KITCHEN

CRISPY SKIN PORK BELLY WITH PINEAPPLE AND CHILLI RELISH, LIME MAYONNAISE

SERVES 4

PINEAPPLE RELISH

25 ml extra virgin olive oil
2 spring onions, finely sliced (including white)
¼ Spanish onion, finely chopped
½ green capsicum, cut into 2 cm pieces
2 green chillies, finely sliced
2 cassette chillies*, finely sliced
50 g (⅓ cup) palm sugar
1 tablespoon brown sugar
1 tablespoon caster sugar
1 small pineapple, cut into 2 cm pieces
50 ml red wine vinegar
few pinches smoked paprika
few pinches chilli flakes or cayenne pepper

LIME MAYONNAISE

2 free-range egg yolks
1 free-range egg
1 teaspoon dijon mustard
250 ml (1 cup) vegetable oil
1 lime, juiced and zested
boiling water

CRISPY SKIN PORK BELLY

1 teaspoon sea salt
½ teaspoon chilli flakes
pinch of white pepper
½ teaspoon dried oregano
500 g boneless pork belly, cut into 125 g pieces
  (your butcher can cut it for you)

lettuce
parsley

To make the pineapple relish, place a heavy-bottomed pot over medium heat. Add the oil. Once the oil is hot add the spring onions and Spanish onions, and sweat for 5 minutes. Add the capsicum and cook for 3 minutes. Add the chillies and cook for 2 minutes.

Now add the palm sugar, brown sugar and caster sugar. Cook until the sugar begins to caramelise and the pot smells hot and sweet.

Add the pineapple and any remaining juice. Cook for 5 minutes. Taste, and add the vinegar. Add the spices and season well with sea salt and freshly ground black pepper. Cook until the pineapple has softened, approximately 20 minutes. The relish should be hot and spicy, sweet and intense.

Next, make the lime mayonnaise. Place the egg yolks and whole egg together with the mustard in a food processor. Blend for 5 minutes, until the mixture is very fluffy and rises within the bowl. Gradually pour the oil in a thin stream into the mixture. Once the oil is completely combined test the thickness; the mixture may need more oil.

When the mixture is thick enough to coat the back of the spoon, restart the food processor and add the lime juice and some sea salt to taste. Gently add a little boiling water to stabilise the mixture and make it creamy. Fold the lime zest through the mixture.

To prepare the pork combine the sea salt, chilli flakes, white pepper and dried oregano in a small bowl. Rub the salt mixture into the pork. Over a medium–high heat on a barbecue or grill (charcoal if possible), lay the pork down on the grill and cook for 3 minutes on each side until the top is quite crispy and the bottom is juicy.

Serve straight away in a crunchy roll spread with pineapple relish, then lettuce, parsley and lime mayonnaise on top. You can also serve the pork belly on rice, couscous or any of your favourite bases!

Cassette chillies go by other names as well; they are the very small, very powerful chillies.

Food truck owner Dave has worked in the food industry for many years, and spent just as many travelling around the world gaining ideas and inspiration for his passion, that is, to cook modern street food using only the freshest ethically sourced produce.

The result is his Digging for Fire BBQ Kitchen food truck, which serves a range of dishes with flavour influences from all over the globe. The menu includes such dishes as slow-cooked smoky lamb shoulder served with a tahini dressing, North African barbecue chicken with tagine spices and Damo's harissa (Damo is Dave's trusty sidekick). This is world food that defies categorisation, with the only common thread being that all dishes are cooked with fire – a wood-fire barbecue grill using Australian mallee root charcoal, to be exact.

Dishes that bear cute names like 'Mary had a little lamb' and 'This little piggy went to the market' are perhaps a giveaway that Dave opened this truck partly to spend more time with his young family. The adventures of being on the road, at festivals and events are also good reasons for Dave, who claims to have once cooked for Pavarotti.

And speaking of music, that's how the truck got its name. While searching for potential truck names the Pixies song 'Dig For Fire' came on in the background. No need to look any further, the name was set.

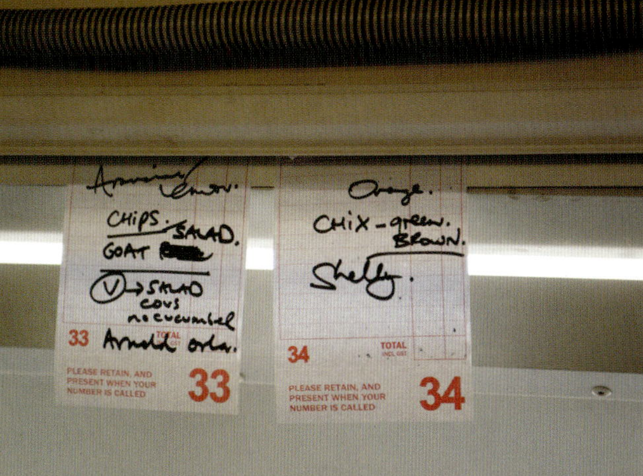

CHIPS - SALAD
GOAT
SALAD
COUS
no cucumber
33 Arnold Ordi
TOTAL
33
PLEASE RETAIN, AND
PRESENT WHEN YOUR
NUMBER IS CALLED
Orange.
CHIX - green.
BROWN.
Shelby.
34 TOTAL
(INCL GST)
34
PLEASE RETAIN, AND
PRESENT WHEN YOUR
NUMBER IS CALLED

GRUMBLE TUMMS

Sometimes the best ideas come to you out of the blue, when your mind is at rest, unimpeded by reason or logic. Perhaps this is how Grumble Tumms owner Vanessa woke up one day with the idea to start a food truck. Though she had only ever cooked for her family and had never owned her own business, Vanessa wanted to create a food truck with a difference – serving food made with Australian native meats like crocodile, wallaby, emu and kangaroo, and Australian native bush herbs.

Even among Australians, native meats may get a lukewarm reception, so Vanessa's solution was to camouflage them in the country's beloved dishes of meat pies and burgers. She emphasises that crocodile, emu and kangaroo meats all have a very low fat content, while being high in protein and iron, so they're healthier options as well as being local products.

The Chinese also believe that crocodile meat can be very beneficial for those suffering from asthma and other lung conditions because it assists the body to repair damaged lung tissue.

CROCODILE SPRING ROLLS

MAKES 30 MINI SPRING ROLLS

100 g vermicelli rice noodles
½ tablespoon olive oil
3 teaspoons ginger, crushed
1 teaspoon garlic, crushed
4 spring onions, sliced
500 g crocodile mince*
¼ cabbage, shredded
2 carrots, peeled and grated
2 teaspoons fish sauce
4 tablespoons soy sauce
1 tablespoon worcestershire sauce
1 teaspoon fresh coriander leaves, chopped
30 sheets pre-prepared spring roll pastry*

Begin by putting the vermicelli rice noodles in a bowl. Cover them with boiling water and leave to soak until softened.

In a deep frying pan or wok heat the oil and sauté the ginger, garlic and spring onions for 2–3 minutes. Add the crocodile mince and cook over medium heat, until the mince is white (note: crocodile mince will not brown over medium heat). Add the shredded cabbage and grated carrots. Cover with the lid and cook over low heat for 10 minutes, stirring often.

Add the fish sauce, soy sauce, worcestershire sauce and chopped coriander leaves to the frying pan or wok and cook for 3–4 minutes.

Drain the noodles and chop them into 2–3 cm lengths. Stir through the crocodile mince mixture.

To make the spring rolls, place one spring roll pastry sheet diagonally in front of you and spoon approximately 1 tablespoon of the spring roll mixture on the bottom corner. Fold the bottom corner up over the filling, continue rolling until you are level with the next two corners, and then fold the corners inwards over the filling.

Continue rolling to the end of the sheet, sealing with an equal mix of flour/water. Make sure the spring roll is tight as you are wrapping or it will fall apart when you are cooking it. Continue with the next sheet until you've used up all of the mixture.

The crocodile spring rolls can be shallow fried in a frying pan or deep fried in a wok. You can also freeze them for up to 6 months.

Gluten-free alternative

** Use rice-paper spring roll pastry sheets. For best results cook immediately (this version of the recipe is not really suitable to freeze).*

** If you can't purchase crocodile mince, you can use chicken mince instead.*

GRUMBLETUMMS
Hot Chips 4°
Hot Dogs 4°
Croc Burger 10°
Chicken Schnitzel Roll 8°
Bushmans Beef Pie 5°
COLD Drinks $2.50

DANGER
CROCODILES
NO
SWIMMING

KANGAROO
EMU
CROCODILE

Croc Bites 3 for 5°
Croc Burger 10°
Chicken Schnitzel Roll 8°
Bushmans Beef Pie 5°
Hot Chips 4° Hot Dogs 4°

JAFE JAFFLES

RHUBARB, MASCARPONE AND VANILLA BEAN JAFFLE

SERVES 4

400 g (3¼ cups) fresh rhubarb, stalks trimmed
2 tablespoons raw sugar
1 vanilla bean, split lengthways
80 ml (⅓ cup) water
l00 g mascarpone
100 g salted butter, softened
8 thick slices brioche

Cut the rhubarb into 2 cm pieces and place into a saucepan with the sugar, vanilla bean and water. Simmer for 5 minutes, or until tender. Drain the excess juice through a fine sieve and discard the vanilla bean. Cool the mixture completely.

Preheat the jaffle maker until the green light switches on. Butter one side of each slice of brioche and place 4 slices in the jaffle maker, buttered side down.

Mix the mascarpone through the cooled rhubarb mixture and spread evenly over the 4 slices of brioche in the jaffle maker. Cover with remaining brioche slices, making sure that the buttered side is facing up.

Close the jaffle maker lid and cook for 3 minutes or until the brioche is golden and crisp.

Serve immediately with an extra dollop of mascarpone and fresh rhubarb.

Take a slice of cheese between two pieces of bread and toast until melted. Simple! And yet the satisfaction this basic meal provides is immeasurable. So it's only fitting that this humble treasure, the jaffle (or toastie), can now come to you served out of a truck.

Armed with an ex-military VW van, owner Luke takes the jaffle to another level. Of course, there's the basic baked bean and cheese variety, but Luke has also created the 'Sophie Monk', named after the Australian singer, made with monkfish, Japanese edamame and creamy mornay sauce; and the 'Jafael Nadal', filled with roast pumpkin, quinoa, feta, marjoram and pine nuts – a real winner just like the tennis player!

CAFE

CAFE
TOASTED
SANDWICHES
COFFEE & TEA
DRINKS
VANILLA ICECREAM

Jafé Jaffles
is an official
Daffodil
Day
Supporter
JAFFLE'S
FOOD TRUCK
JAFFLES
BPZ·45X
JAFFLES

JAFFLES

THE LITTLE CAKE TIN

BLUE MOON

MAKES 6 × 125 ML DESSERT GLASSES,
OR 12 × 65 ML SHOT GLASSES

BLUEBERRY COULIS
500 g (3⅓ cup) blueberries
150 g (⅔ cup) caster sugar
1 tablespoon lemon juice

PANNA COTTA
375 ml (1½ cups) cream
375 ml (1 ½ cups) full cream milk
1 teaspoon vanilla bean paste or 1 whole vanilla bean
115 g (½ cup) caster sugar
2 tablespoons boiling water
1½ teaspoons gelatine powder

To make the blueberry coulis place the blueberries, caster sugar and lemon juice in a small saucepan and cook over medium heat until the mixture thickens, about 10 or 15 minutes. Strain the mixture through a fine mesh strainer to catch the skins. Cool completely.

To make the panna cotta place the cream and milk in a saucepan. Add the vanilla bean paste or use a small sharp knife to split the whole vanilla bean lengthways, then scrape the seeds from inside the bean and add the seeds and bean to the saucepan. Slowly bring to the boil over medium heat. As soon as it starts to boil remove from the heat and set aside to cool for 10 minutes.

If you've used a whole vanilla bean discard it from the cream mixture. Add the sugar and place the saucepan over a low heat. Cook, stirring, for 5 minutes or until the sugar dissolves.

Place 2 tablespoons of boiling water in a small heatproof bowl. Sprinkle the gelatin powder over it and stir until dissolved. Stir the gelatine mixture into the cream mixture until combined. Pour the mixture through a fine sieve to remove any gelatine lumps.

Pour the cream mixture into 6 × 125 ml dessert glasses or 12 × 65 ml shot glasses for these mini desserts. Refrigerate for 4 hours.

Slowly pour a thin layer of cooled blueberry coulis on top of the panna cotta and serve.

Sometimes it's not about breaking rules or breaking new ground. Sometimes it's as simple as doing what you love and doing it well enough to share with the world. This is exactly what friends Samantha and Rosalie have done.

The lovely ladies behind the Little Cake Tin met on their children's first day of school and have been friends ever since. With a shared love of baking, they complement each other perfectly, retaining 'other' careers while getting together for festivals, events and catering gigs to bake up delicious sweet things.

Their gorgeous lemon-coloured vintage trailer, which resembles an oversized cake tin, was custom-fitted by Rosalie's husband. With matching pillows on a side bench, this food truck set-up is so beautifully decorated it would put some bricks-and-mortar businesses to shame.

The Little Cake Tin

CASSATA
chocolate cake layered with orange chocolate

THE SWEET AND THE SALTY
almond based fresh cheese cake with salted caramel

MERINGUE TANG BANG
lemon curd cheese cake topped with fluffy meringue

BLUE MOON
blueberry panna cotta GF

LEMON TWIST
lemon poppy seed bundt cake

THE CRUMBLER
apricot crumble

MOROCCAN DELIGHT
pistachio cake GF

The Little Cake Tin

THE LITTLE MUSHROOM CO.

The Little Mushroom Co.'s mushroom burgers are so juicy and delicious, even the most dedicated carnivore is likely to line up for them. And that's because owner Bryan carefully selects, trials and scrutinises every ingredient before it makes it onto one of his burgers.

Looking at his hand-painted, modest little black caravan, you'd never guess that Bryan worked in foreign affairs and spent several years in Turkey on diplomatic postings. Neither would you guess that he was a sales expert for major Australian audio-visual company JB Hi-Fi.

The origin of Bryan's mushroom 'obsession' stems from his propensity to take on any task with dogged dedication. During a road trip across the States he ate only fast food and not surprisingly, the medical diagnosis following the trip forced Bryan to reconsider his nutrition and lifestyle. The humble mushroom was his answer.

At first glance the menu may seem quite modest with only a few items on it, including 'the Mexican', 'the Greek', 'the Vegan' and 'the Gluten-free', but you can also order just grilled haloumi, saganaki or Mexican corn on its own. In any case, the flavours are big!

By the way, occasionally Bryan also features dishes without mushrooms (see recipe below). But don't fret, the same care and dedication has gone into them as with all his prime menu items.

RATATOUILLE BURGER

At the Little Mushroom Co. they are very big on maximising flavours and textures, so wherever possible use organic produce. They purposely cut their vegetables into irregular sizes and cook them in batches, allowing some to catch on the grill to create a lovely smoky flavour.

The sweetness in their burgers comes from sweating the onions in the oven at a very low heat.

SERVES 6

1 whole garlic bulb
2 onions (white, brown or Spanish)
4 ripe capsicums (red, green or yellow)
3 zucchinis
4 tomatoes (roma or similar)
extra virgin olive oil
½ bottle passata sauce
½ cup red wine
splash of red wine vinegar
**dried Italian herbs (or a combination of oregano,
   coriander and a little rosemary works well)**
pinch of smoked paprika
bay leaf (optional)

rocket leaves
splash of balsamic vinegar
parmesan, grated

6 ciabatta buns or similar

Preheat fan-forced oven to 150ºC (170ºC conventional/Gas 3). Cut the top off the garlic bulb (exposing just the tips of the cloves) and place it, together with 2 of the whole capsicums, on a tray. Drizzle olive oil liberally over them. Add the whole onions to the same tray, or in a separate smaller tray, and put all of the vegetables in the oven. Cook for approximately 30 minutes (check the garlic bulb after 20 minutes; it may need to be removed earlier).

Put the onions, whole, in the oven. Drizzle some olive oil over 2 capsicums (also whole) and put in the oven as well. Cook onions and capsicums for about 30 minutes.

Halve the zucchinis lengthways. Drizzle the zucchinis and the remaining capsicums with a little olive oil and salt, and grill them on a barbecue or on a flat plate with exposed griddles. (The taste is much better on a barbecue.) Turn them when they start to char.

Put the capsicums from the grill into a bowl and cover with foil or plastic wrap while the capsicums are still hot, to allow them to sweat. After a few minutes peel the skins off the capsicums, remove and discard the stem and seeds, and rip into irregular but still large pieces. Cut the zucchinis into large irregular pieces as well.

Remove the garlic bulb from the oven and, when cooled a little, squeeze the garlic from each clove. Remove the skin from the onions and cut into irregular bits (they will have separated beautifully after being in the oven).

In a large pan, over a medium flame, heat some olive oil and add the capsicum, zucchini, onion and garlic. Cook for a couple of minutes, stirring. Pour in the passata, red wine and red wine vinegar and continue to stir.

Add the herbs, paprika and bay leaf, and cover. Reduce to a low heat and cook for 2–4 hours.

When done, toast the buns in a pan or under the grill. Cut them in half and drizzle with a little olive oil. Spoon some ratatouille onto the bun and finish with some rocket, balsamic vinegar and a little parmesan.

If the ratatouille is tasting quite acidic, you can add a little sugar to the vegetables to balance the vinegar.

The ratatouille always tastes much better over the next few days after it has had time to settle and develop its flavours. It will keep in the refrigerator for around a week.

THE
MUSHROOM

THE   LITTLE
Grilled
HALLOUMI
Mushroom
BURGERS
MUSHROOM   CO
thelittlemushroomco
@thelittlemushco
0405 985 000
www.TheLittleMushroomCo.com

TRAILER MADE

CHILLI

This chilli can be used as an accompaniment to all savoury foods.

MAKES 4 × 250 ML JARS

CONFIT GARLIC OIL
250 ml (1 cup) olive oil
24 garlic cloves, peeled

1 kg fresh red chillies
1 whole garlic bulb
200 g caster sugar
150 ml white wine vinegar
1½ tablespoons salt
2 tablespoons ground coriander

Make the confit garlic oil first. Heat the oil in a saucepan over low heat. Once warmed, add the garlic and cook until the garlic softens.

Chop the red chillies (seeds and all) into 1 cm pieces. Put them in a medium-size pot, with all remaining ingredients and 150 ml of the confit garlic oil. Cook over medium heat until the chillies break down.

Allow to cool slightly. Then transfer the mixture to a medium-size bowl and blend using a food processor, until well combined.

You can store the chilli mixture in jars in the refrigerator. It will keep for approximately 1 month. As you use it, top the jar up with the confit garlic oil or oilve oil to prolong the shelf life.

As the daughter of entrepreneurial parents, Trailer Made truck owner Amy is proof that the apple doesn't fall far from the tree. Amy and her former partner Casey, a fine-dining restaurant chef, originally started up a mobile food venture after their inspiring travels in Europe, China and Korea. When they returned to Australia, their aim was to create high-quality food with style, despite it being served from a truck.

Although Amy and Casey recently parted ways, Amy continues the business, cruising around Melbourne with a sleek, little black trailer and a fairly subtle logo. The cart carries a quiet elegance and understated style, much like the food it serves.

Indeed, Trailer Made proves that street food doesn't necessarily equate to dude food. The regularly changing menu using seasonal ingredients may include fatayers (Middle Eastern spinach, feta and pine nut parcels), Moroccan soups, grain salads and honey dumplings with cinnamon, lavender and ricotta. All of these items would sit just as comfortably on a high-end restaurant menu.

TRAILERMADE
TRAILERMADE
TRAILERMADE

ARTISAN FOODS
TRAILERMADE
SINCE FOREVER

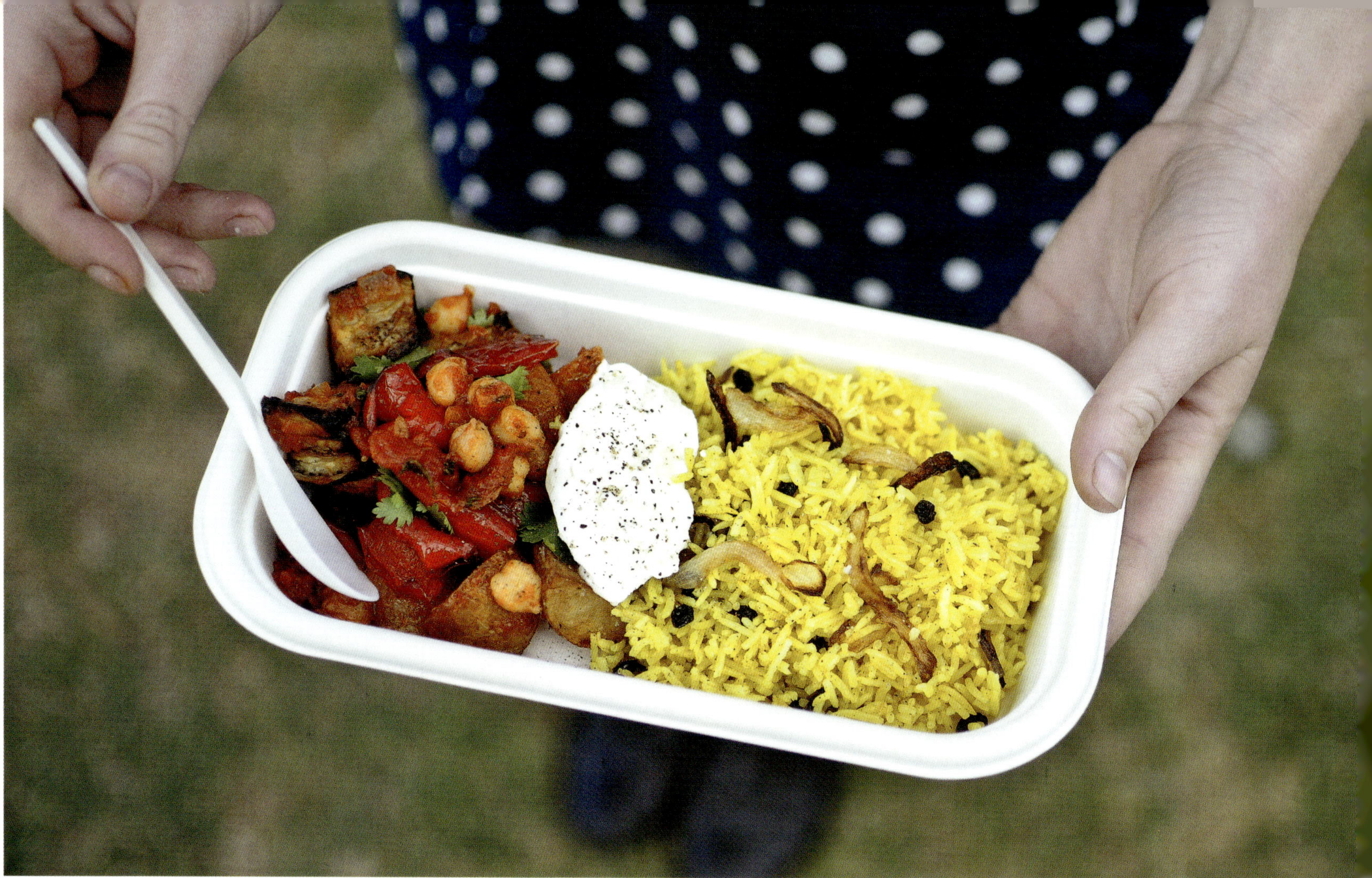

HUNGRY
FOODTRUCK
THIS WAY

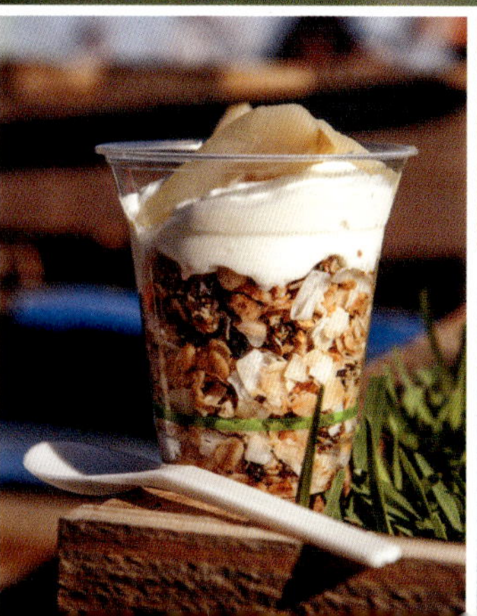

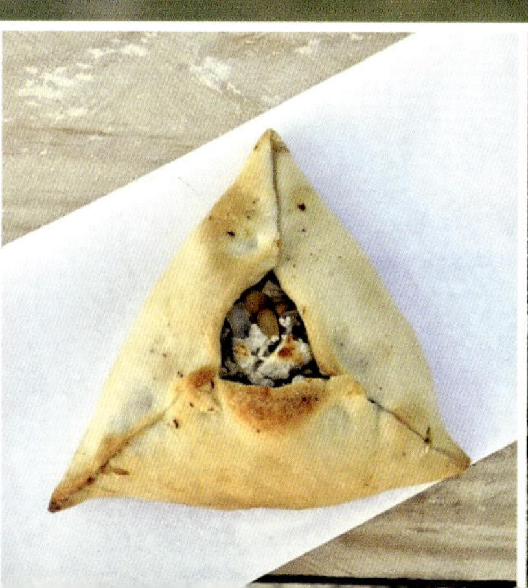

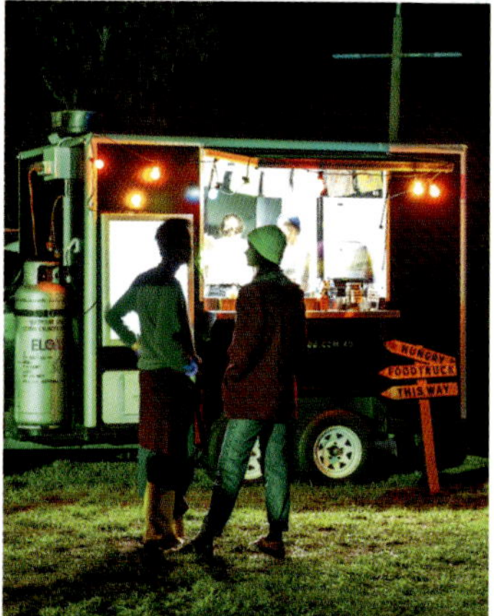

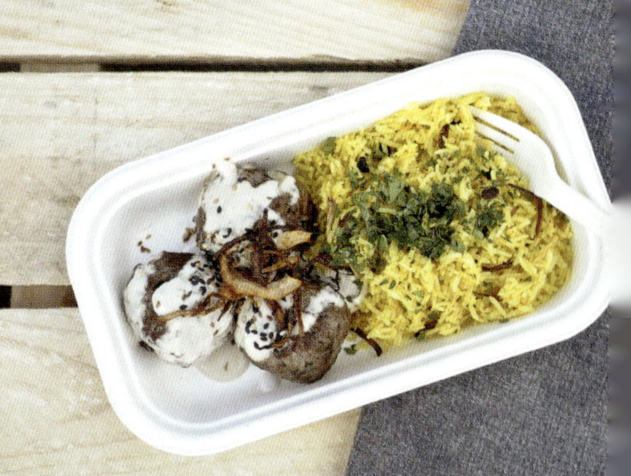

TRAILERMADEFOOD.COM.AU

CHEEKY AUSSIE BITES

AUTUMN MENU

FATAYER
SPINACH, FETTA, PINE NUT PIE
$7

FRIED POTATOES
BEANS (OPTIONAL), TOMATO, CHILLI, HERBS
$10

LAMB KOFTA
SALAD, TAHINI, FRIED ONION, PILAF
$14

ORANGE CAKE
HERBS, OLIVE OIL, PISTACHIO
$6

TRAILER MADE ICED TEA
OUR OWN SPECIAL BLEND
$4

* BYPASS AVAILABLE *

TRAILERMADEFOOD.COM.AU

TRAILERMADEFOOD.COM.AU

VEGGIE PATCH VAN

ZUCCHINI, FETA AND CHICKPEA FRITTERS

MAKES 4 FRITTERS

100 g (¾ cup) zucchini, grated
80 g tinned chickpeas
40 g (¼ cup) feta, crumbled
50 g (½ cup) parmesan, grated
1 tablespoon fresh dill, chopped
1 tablespoon fresh mint, chopped
2 teaspoon lemon zest
2 spring onions, finely chopped
40 ml olive oil

BATTER
40 g chickpea flour
1 egg
60 ml (¼ cup) cold water
½ teaspoon cumin powder
pinch cayenne pepper
¼ teaspoon baking powder
30 g (¼ cup) sunflower seeds

Place grated zucchini in a clean tea towel and squeeze, releasing as much liquid as possible. Transfer zucchini to a medium-size bowl and mix with the chickpeas, feta, parmesan, dill, mint, lemon zest and spring onions. Season with salt and pepper.

In a separate medium-size bowl, add all the ingredients for the batter. Mix to combine. Once ingredients form a smooth batter, add the zucchini mixture and gently fold it into the batter. Refrigerate for 20 minutes.

Heat the olive oil in a heavy-based frying pan. When the oil is hot add large ladles of the batter to it and cook each fritter for 3 minutes, then flip and cook for another 3 minutes, or until golden brown and cooked through.

We should all take a leaf out of the Veggie Patch Van's 'how to live with a cleaner conscience' handbook. This vintage Winnebago – or 'Spud' as it has been endearingly dubbed – is proof that it is possible to run a successful business with sustainable resources and a minimal environmental footprint. 'Spud' has solar panels attached to its roof and a motor that runs on vegetable oil used previously to fry up food. The van's wood exterior is a collection of sustainable plantation pine boards, as well as random bits of materials found on roadsides, at demolition sites and in junkyards. Boxes of herbs attached to the side panels are not only decorative, but functional for garnishes, too. Everything down to the packaging used to serve the food has been carefully considered to ensure minimal wastage and maximum biodegradability.

All of these environmental efforts are certainly inspiring, but for many customers this may be a secondary reason to chase up the truck. The primary reason is the food! The original Veggie Patch team – made up of friends Milenka, Karl, Zoran and Georgie – has created a delicious and completely vegetarian menu using only locally sourced and seasonal produce. A staple favourite is the zucchini, feta and chickpea fritter burger, while the haloumi burger served with coleslaw, beetroot, relish, chipotle and bourbon barbecue sauce is a close follow-up. Add to this a bowl of crunchy sweet potato chips that come with vegan basil mayonnaise, and you can chomp down on your meal guilt-free and happy in the knowledge you're doing both yourself and your planet a favour.

CHEEKY AUSSIE BITES

WILD HORSE CAFE

ESPRESSO MARTINI

SERVES 1

60 ml (¼ cup) fresh espresso shot
30 ml vanilla vodka
30 ml Kahlua
ice

espresso beans

Pour all ingredients into a shaker. Shake with ice and strain. Add fresh espresso beans for garnish.

COCONUT MOJITO

SERVES 1

1 fresh young coconut, cut to allow a 5 × 5 cm opening at the top
60 ml (¼ cup) rum (e.g. Sailor Jerry's)
fresh mint
ice

Cut a 5 × 5 cm opening at the top of the coconut using a meat cleaver. Tip out or drink the coconut liquid inside. Add the rum, mint and a small amount of ice. Stir.

It tastes better with a little umbrella!

'If the cafe won't come to Muhammad, then Muhammad must make his own coffee.' So goes the old proverb, well, sort of … it's one that springs to mind when thinking of Kat and Christine, the two savvy gals behind Wild Horse Cafe.

As dedicated music festival-goers, Kat and Christine felt that festivals and good coffee should go hand in hand. But after going to various music festivals only to be stuck with average hot java, they started taking their own plunger coffee with them. They quickly realised they were onto something when coffee requests from other festival-goers started to pour in, and so the Wild Horse Cafe food truck was born.

The food truck itself is a vintage caravan that Kat and Christine found on eBay and renovated themselves. These days their coffee plunger is long gone, and they now have a professional coffee machine and attitude to match. They also serve juices, fresh coconuts (in season), a select number of delicious cocktails, and gluten-free snacks baked by the entrepreneurial chicks themselves.

CHEEKY AUSSIE BITES

WILD HORSE CAFE

H.M.V STEREOPHONIC

coffee
coconuts
iced latte
raw smoothies
gluten free
vegan treats

YOGURDDICTION

On first impressions, Yogurddiction may just seem like a modern version of Mr Whippy, Australia's iconic ice-cream food truck. But Yogurddiction owner Elle, who studied film production in LA, firmly belongs to the new generation of the food truck fleet.

Instead of Mr Whippy's rather dubious tinkling tune that rings out of the truck and lures innocent children to the streets like the Pied Piper, Elle communicates solely through social media, announcing her presence at festivals, functions or her street locations.

Originally from Singapore, Elle only puts the best ingredients into her frozen yoghurt, using skim milk and locally sourced products. There are usually two basic yoghurt flavours with up to 32 different toppings that can be added to suit your fancy. The best part of owning a food truck for Elle is that with just a few other food-truck friends, they can create a mini festival wherever they go. It's also super-easy to set up and pack up!

PLAIN OL' NATURAL!

SERVES 30 × 120 G TUBS

1 kg (4 cups) natural yogurt
5 litres (20 cups) skim milk
1 litre (4 cups) apple juice
30 g raw sugar
100 g manuka honey

Simply mix all the ingredients in a mixer or food processor until smooth and creamy.

Pour mixture into little tubs and pop them into the freezer.

For flavour variations you can use fruit purees or fresh fruit and blend them with the original ingredients.

EUROPEAN FOODIE PASSPORT

THE BRÛLÉE CART

LAVENDER AND HONEY CRÈME BRÛLÉE

SERVES 6

500 ml (2 cups) thickened or whipping cream
1 tablespoon dried cooking lavender*
3 tablespoons honey
6 large free range-egg yolks
cassonade sugar* or caster sugar (for the topping)

Pour the cream into a saucepan over medium heat. Bring it to the boil then remove from heat.

Add the dried cooking lavender to the cream and stir through for 1 minute. Leave the mixture to infuse for at least 30 minutes, stirring occasionally.

Strain the mixture using a sieve to separate the lavender from the liquid.

Preheat a fan-forced oven to 135°C (155°C conventional/Gas 1).

Return the saucepan to the stove. Over low heat bring the mixture to a simmer. Remove from heat and slowly stir in the honey.

Beat the egg yolks together in a bowl, slowly adding a small amount of the cream mixture at a time, until it is all combined. Pour the mixture into the ramekins, then place the ramekins into a large baking dish. Pour hot water into the baking dish until it reaches half way up the ramekins, to make a bain-marie. Carefully place the baking dish in the oven and cook for 45 minutes.

Remove the ramekins from the oven. The crème brûlée will be firm, but still a little wobbly when tapped. Cool for 15 minutes then cover and place in the refrigerator for a minimum of 4 hours.

Remove the ramekins from the fridge. Sprinkle a light layer of cassonade sugar on top and caramelise with a kitchen blowtorch to make a toffee. While the toffee is still setting, garnish with a little dried lavender.

Dried cooking lavender is available from specialty food stores.

Cassonade sugar is also available from specialty food stores.

Brothers Jack and Bart learned how to cook from a very young age, thanks to their mother, a keen and talented cook. With such an avid interest in food instilled in them, entrepreneurialism seemed a natural step forward for these brothers. So at ages 15 and 13 respectively, and a trailer cart in tow, Jack and Bart attended music and food festivals with their parents, selling freshly made Belgian waffles. It was a far cooler introduction to working life compared to the usual tour of duty at McDonald's that many of us endured!

Their waffle cart is occasionally still in operation, but Jack realised this cart requires a lot of electricity to run productively. So with a second cart that Bart and their father fitted out, Jack reached out to his friends and followers with a crowd-funding campaign to cover the remaining start-up costs for his next venture: the delicate French treat, the crème brûlée. These delicious desserts could be prepared in an off-site kitchen, leaving only the theatre of torching the sugar crust to be done during service.

Using the best of local ingredients, Jack is constantly experimenting with different combinations. The Brûlée Cart offers flavours such as salted caramel and French vanilla, rocky road, lemon meringue, lavender and honey, caramel popcorn, pistachio … the possibilities are endless. But nothing compares to the divine sound of a spoon decisively cracking open the sugar crust of a crème brûlée – magic.

Crème Brûlée
Flavours
FRENCH
VANILLA
CHOCOLATE
SALTED
CARAMEL
& POPCORN
THE
Brûlée
CART

Crème Brûlée
Brûlée
CART
BrûléeCart
S51 195

Crème Brûlée
Brûlée
CART

DELECTABALLS

They're not ashamed to admit it. In fact, bright lettering on their award-winning truck design shouts it out loud and proud – they like big balls! And that's no lie. Before you raise an eyebrow, let me clarify, we're talking about edible balls, er … meatballs to be precise. With such open declarations, it's clear that Delectaballs truck owners David and Christine have their tongues firmly placed in their cheeks.

Between them they have a fair share of hospitality experience, but when the couple decided to start up their food truck business,

David consulted his nonna for authentic Italian recipes he remembers fondly from his childhood.

On board their truck – affectionately called 'Mr Darcy' – the self-proclaimed meatball masterminds offer such dishes as 'The Taj', an Indian butter chicken meatball served in a bun with sour cream and a papadum; and the 'Ceasar's balls', a Caesar salad–inspired open wrap with pork and bacon balls, lettuce, egg and croutons. On occasion they will even have some sweet balls on board, such as the apple cinnamon balls drowned in custard.

BUTTER CHICKEN MEATBALLS

SERVES 4

CHICKEN MEATBALLS

2 tablespoons olive oil, for baking tray
500 g chicken thigh mince
1 egg
40 g (½ cup) breadcrumbs
1 teaspoon salt
½ teaspoon white pepper
1 teaspoon sage
1 teaspoon garlic, crushed
1 brown onion, finely diced

BUTTER CHICKEN SAUCE

½ white onion, finely diced
2 tablespoons butter
2 teaspoons lemon juice
½ tablespoon ginger, grated
½ tablespoon garlic, crushed
¼ teaspoon ground fenugreek
1 teaspoon garam masala
1 teaspoon chilli powder
1 teaspoon ground cumin
1 bay leaf
600 ml tomato passata
125 ml (½ cup) chicken stock
125 ml (½ cup) thickened cream

To make the chicken meatballs preheat a fan-forced oven to 120ºC (140ºC conventional/Gas 1). Drizzle a baking tray with olive oil.

In a large bowl combine the chicken mince and all other ingredients, and mix by hand until well combined. Using an ice-cream scoop, form balls about 4 cm in diameter. With slightly wet hands, finish off the balls by gently rolling them and lining them on the tray to form a grid, with each ball touching each other.

Bake for 20 minutes, until the meatballs are firm to the touch. Allow to cool.

Next, make the butter chicken sauce. In a medium-size saucepan, sauté the onion until softened. Add the butter, lemon juice, ginger, garlic, fenugreek, garam masala, chilli powder, cumin and bay leaf. Cook and continue to stir for 1–2 minutes.

Pour in the passata and chicken stock, continue to stir. Let the sauce reduce for 3–4 minutes.

Turn off the heat and add the cream. Stir to combine. Season with salt and pepper.

Place the freshly cooked chicken meatballs into butter chicken sauce, and gently heat for 15 minutes.

The butter chicken sauce will begin to thicken and coat the balls. Once it has thickened, it is ready to serve.

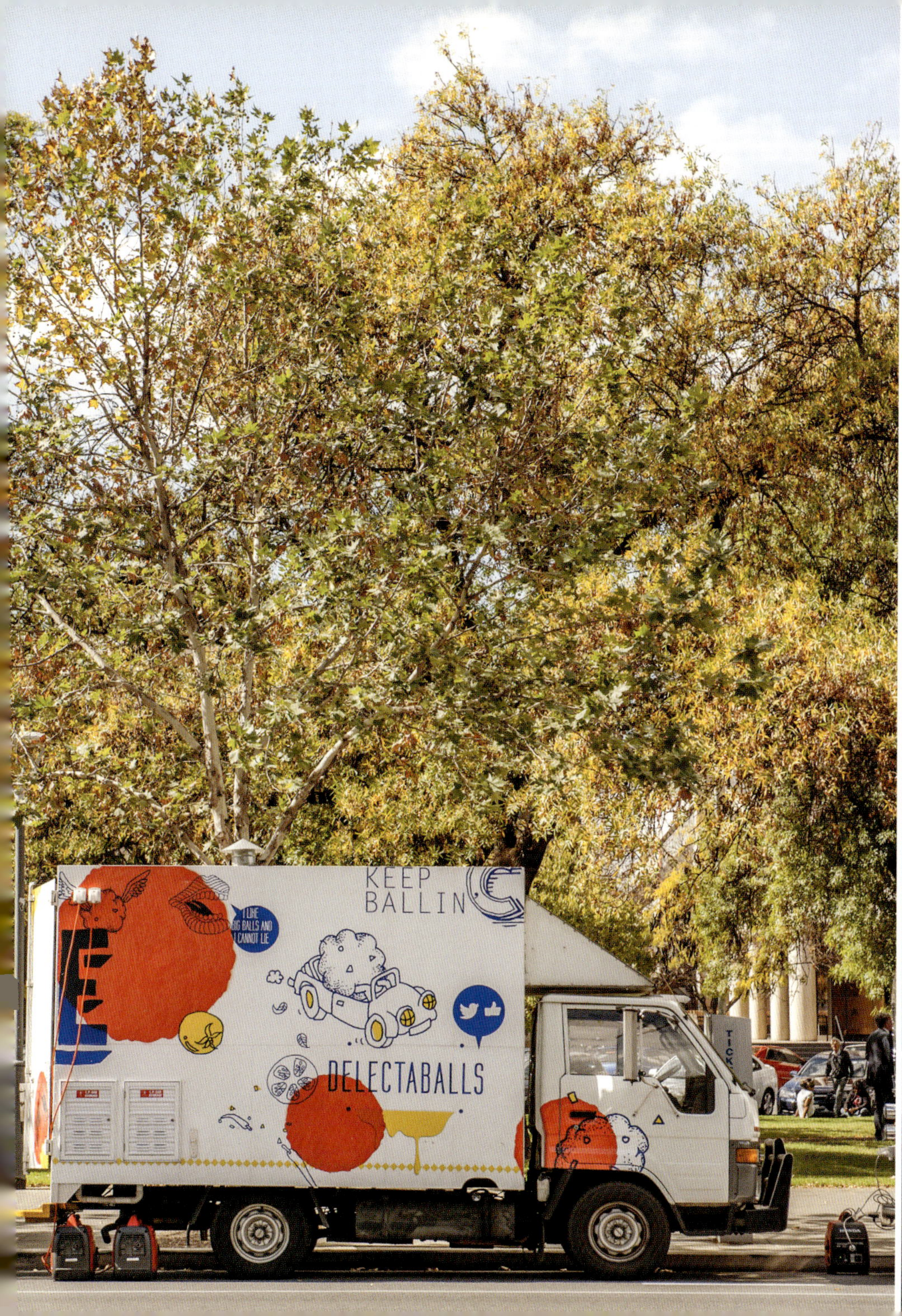
KEEP
BALLIN
DELECTABALLS

DELECTABALLS

TABASCO
TABASCO
PIRI PIRI
TABASCO

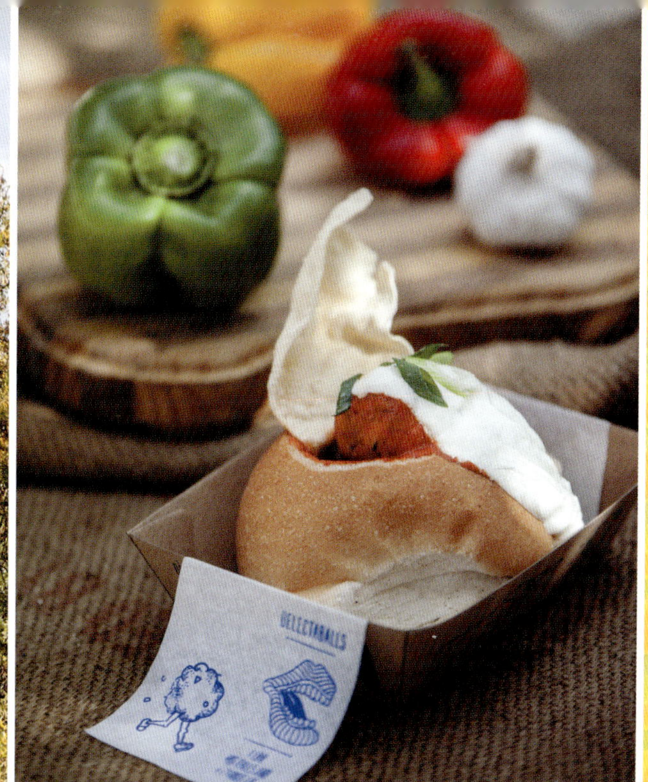

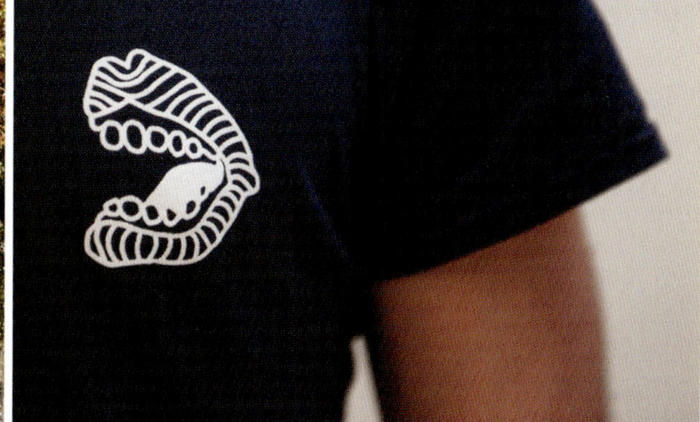

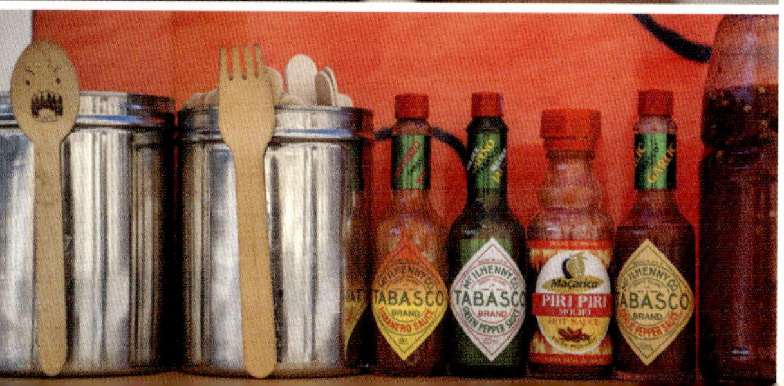

DELECTABALLS

DELECTABALLS

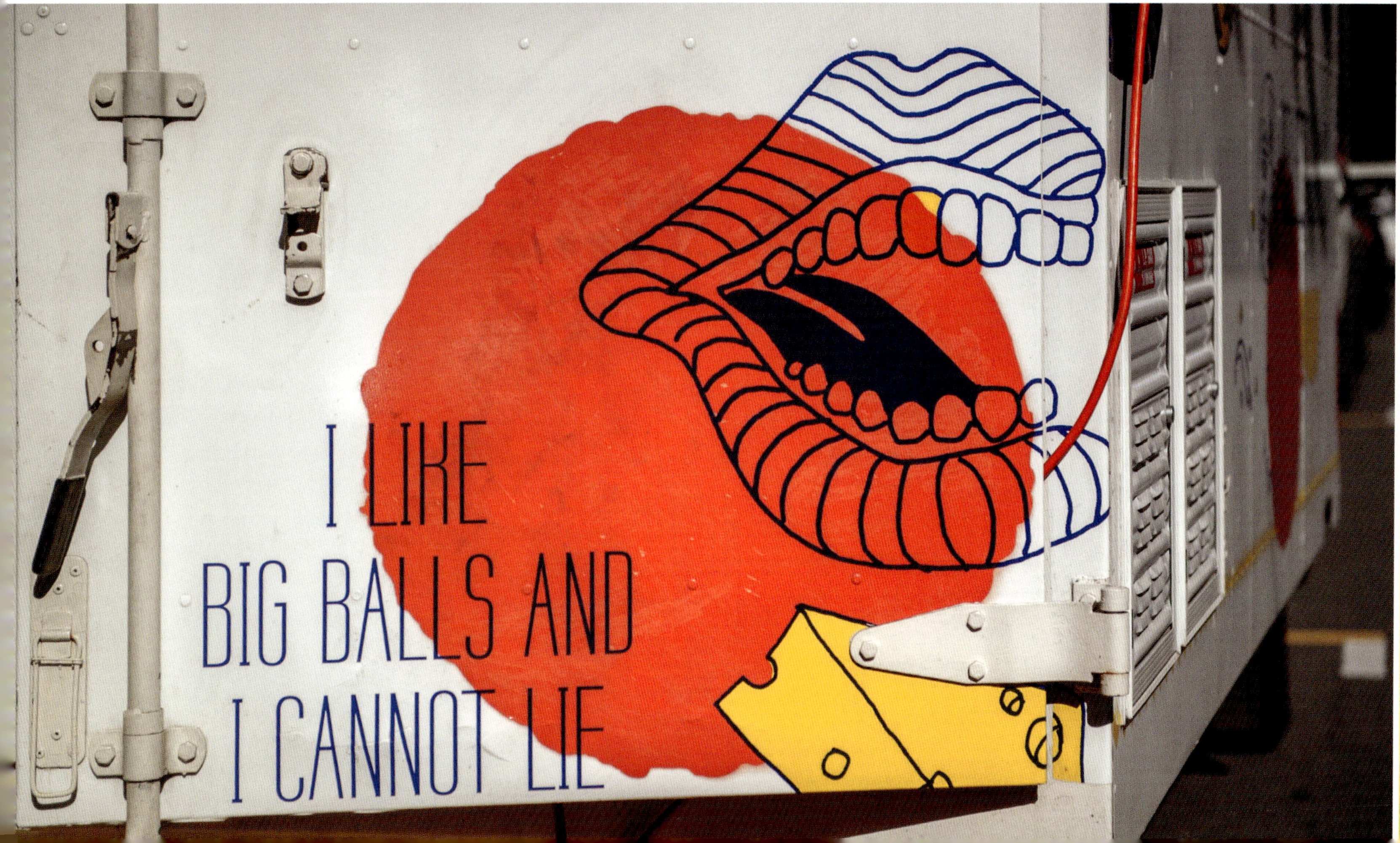

I LIKE
BIG BALLS AND
I CANNOT LIE

GREEK STREET FOOD

Greek Street Food owners George and Flora have been in the food industry for more than 20 years. They are still co-owners of Piraeus Blues, a culinary institution located on Brunswick Street, one of Melbourne's most famous cultural strips.

Seeking a lifestyle change, friendlier hospitality hours and a better life/work balance, George saw the potential for a food truck selling souvlakis, the quintessential Greek street snack, the way it's done in Greece, with fresh hot chips rolled into them. The quirky menu features 'Bahh', 'Oink' and 'Cluck' (hopefully no explanations needed), all served in souvlakis with potato chips. Their version sees oregano-seasoned potato chips rolled into specially sourced pita breads. Vegetarians are also catered for with a choice of salads and a falafel 'souva'.

BEETROOT AND KOLIVA (PEARL BARLEY) SALAD

SERVES 4

1 kg whole beetroots
90 g (¾ cup) slivered almonds
110 g (½ cup) pearl barley (or quinoa)
1 bunch spring onions
2 handfuls rocket leaves
2 garlic cloves, finely chopped
handful fresh mint leaves, finely shredded
olive oil
balsmaic vinegar

YOGHURT MINT DRESSING

100 ml plain Greek yoghurt
¼ teaspoon dry mint leaves
pinch of salt
dash of lemon juice

Preheat a fan-forced oven to 200ºC (220°C conventional/Gas 7).

In a saucepan, cook the whole beetroots (skin on) in plenty of water, over medium heat, until soft. If the beetroot are large, this can take up to 1½ hours. Once cooked, remove them from the water and allow them to cool until they are easy to handle, then remove the skins. The skin should peel away easily. Also remove any firm bits. Cut the beetroot into cubes and set aside to cool completely.

Spread the slivered almonds evenly on a tray lined with baking paper. Cook them in the oven until golden brown, for approximately 15–20 minutes.

Cook the pearl barley (or quinoa) in boiling water for about 10 minutes, drain and run under cold water to cool down. Drain well.

Remove the green leaves from the spring onions and finely slice the white and pale green parts.

Wash the rocket leaves and pat dry with paper towels.

To make the yoghurt mint dressing, combine all the ingredients in a medium bowl.

Place the beetroot in a large bowl. Add half the baked almonds, cooked pearl barley (or quinoa), spring onions, rocket leaves, garlic and mint leaves. Season with salt then drizzle with olive oil and balsamic vinegar to taste.

Mix well, and plate up by drizzling with the yoghurt mint dressing and scattering the remaining almonds on top. Serve and enjoy!

HAPPY CAMPER PIZZA

Thirty-five may seem rather young to be going through a mid-life crisis. But you could forgive Sonia for thinking her husband Remi was on the brink of one when he announced he'd like to take a break from his career as an aeronautical engineer (read: comfortable and stable income) to start up a food truck business. After all, they'd just welcomed their first of three children into the world and Sonia had put her journalism career on hold to care for their newborn. You'd have to be a little crazy to do that, right?

Remi is French with Vietnamese heritage and grew up in Nice, France where pizza food trucks were around long before the craze hit the States.

After moving to Australia and meeting Sonia, Remi saw an opportunity to bring this much-loved French novelty to Melbourne.

They purchased two vintage silver Airstream caravans – one for the food truck business, and the other as their mobile family home while they travelled around Australia selling pizzas. Remi's engineering background certainly came in handy when it came to custom-building the wood-fire oven and converting the mobile kitchen; but the realities of long car travel with young children soon convinced them to return to Melbourne. Happy Camper Pizza continues in Melbourne, at least for the moment.

HAPPY CAMPER SPECIAL – FRESH FIG AND PROSCIUTTO PIZZA WITH GORGONZOLA ON BÉCHAMEL SAUCE

MAKES 4 PIZZAS

PIZZA DOUGH

250 ml (1 cup) lukewarm water
2 teaspoons salt
2 teaspoons dry yeast
1 tablespoon olive oil
450 g high-protein flour or 00 (pizza) flour

BÉCHAMEL SAUCE

40 g butter
2 tablespoons cornflour
250 ml (1 cup) milk
sea salt
cracked pepper
ground nutmeg

240 g grated mozzarella cheese
200 g gorgonzola cheese, broken into small pieces
12 fresh figs, halved (6 half figs per pizza)
1 cup rocket leaves
24 slices parma prosciutto (6 slices per pizza)
balsamic vinegar
extra virgin olive oil

Make the pizza dough first. In a large bowl combine the water, salt and yeast. Add the flour and continue to combine until a dough forms.

Lightly dust a clean work surface with flour or semolina and knead the dough for 5–10 minutes, until smooth. Lightly dust the bowl with flour and place the dough back in it.

Cover with a damp cloth and leave in a warm place to proof for at least 1 hour, until doubled in size.

Dust the work surface again with flour. Divide the dough into 4 portions. Wrap each portion in a damp cloth and allow to proof further. We leave our dough for a minimum of 4 hours, but if pushed for time you can use the dough after 15 minutes.

To make the béchamel sauce, melt the butter in a small saucepan. Stir in the cornflour and cook for 1 minute. Remove the saucepan from the heat and slowly add the milk, using a whisk or wooden spoon to combine. Return the saucepan to a low heat and stir regularly until the sauce begins to thicken. Add salt, pepper and a sprinkle of nutmeg, and set aside to cool.

To prepare the pizzas, preheat the oven to its highest temperature. Lightly dust your work surface with semolina or flour, and roll out a pizza dough portion to your desired thickness.

Lightly spread the pizza base with the béchamel sauce. Sprinkle with shredded mozzarella, then lay some gorgonzola on top. Transfer the pizza onto a preheated pizza stone or baking paper and cook in the oven for 5–10 minutes, until golden and crisp.

Top the cooked pizza with fresh figs, rocket and prosciutto. Drizzle a small amount of balsamic vinegar and olive oil over the top. Season with salt and pepper.

happy
PIZZA
CAMPER

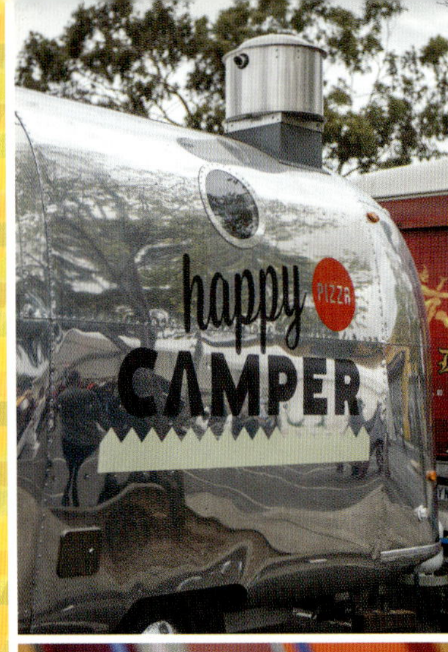

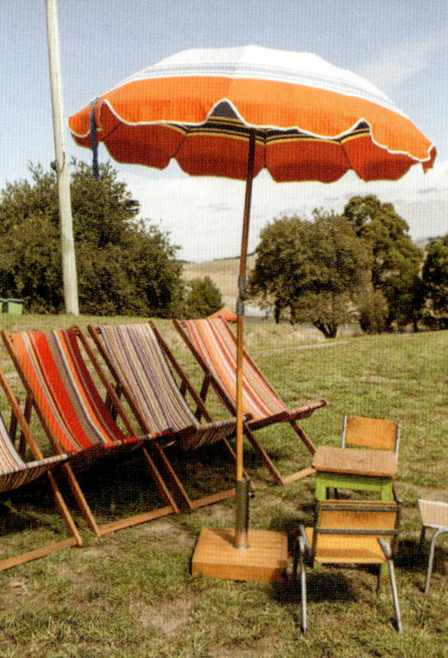

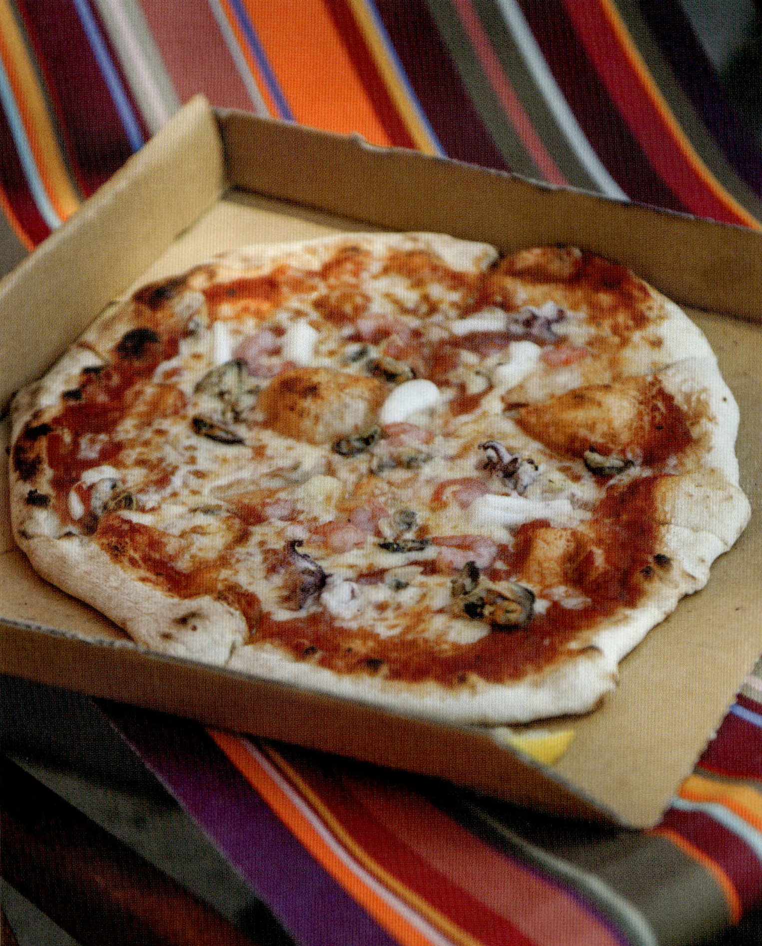

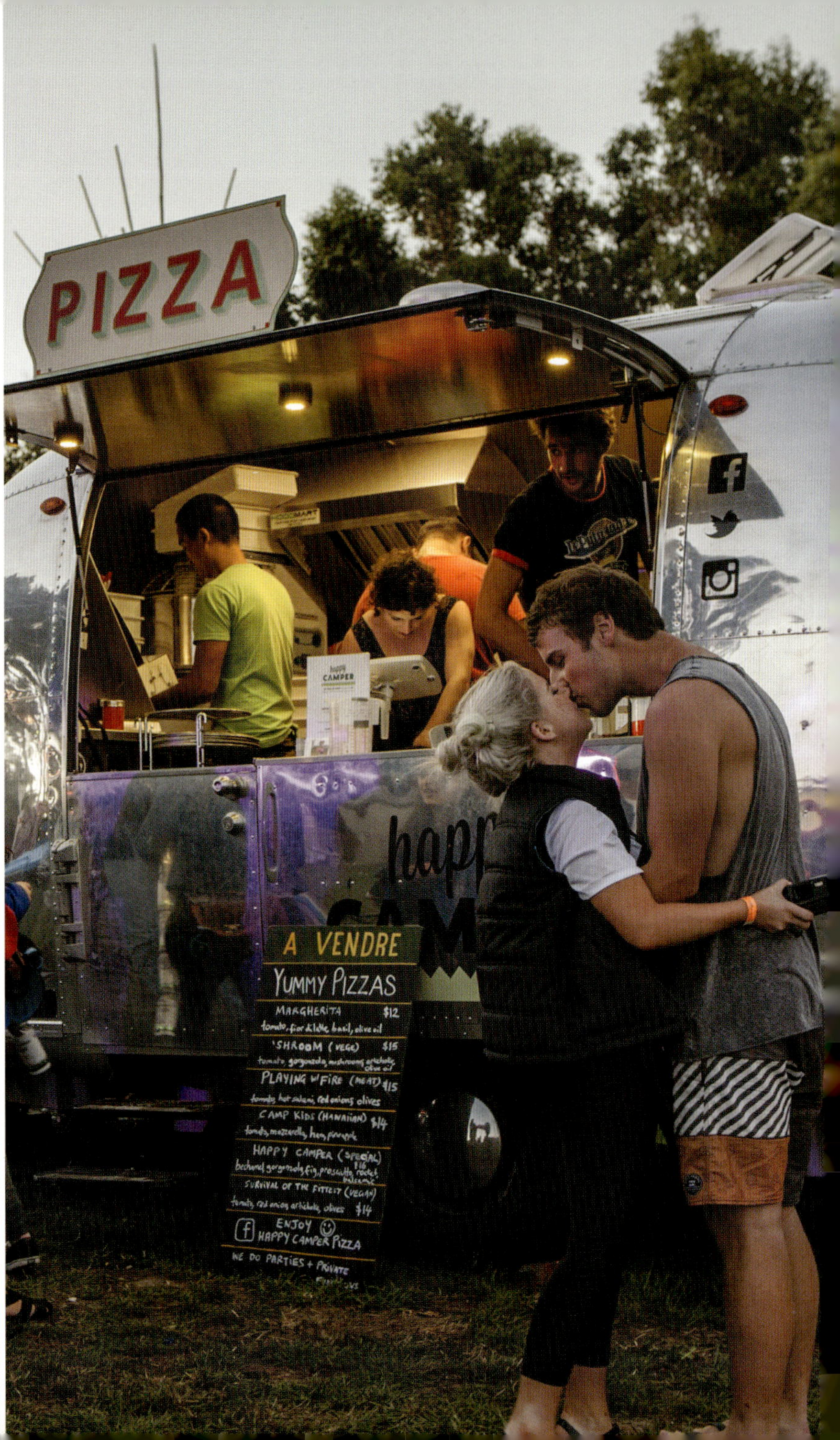
PIZZA
A VENDRE
YUMMY PIZZAS
MARGHERITA $12
'SHROOM (VEGE) $15
PLAYING W/ FIRE (MEAT) $15
tomato, hot salami, red onions, olives
CAMP KIDS (HAWAIIAN) $14
HAPPY CAMPER (SPECIAL) $16
SURVIVAL OF THE FITTEST (VEGAN)
tomato, red onion, artichoke, olives $14
ENJOY
HAPPY CAMPER PIZZA
WE DO PARTIES + PRIVATE

PIZZA WAGON

The young entrepreneurial couple behind Pizza Wagon, Hannah and Zak, met in 2006 while skiing in Canada. Neither Hannah, an English girl from London, nor Zak, an Australian from Melbourne's eastern suburbs, were in the least tempted by a 9am to 5pm lifestyle, so they spent several years travelling around the world, on the way gaining an appreciation of good food and cooking.

According to Hannah, it's not that they are afraid of hard work – they just aren't keen to work hard for something they don't believe in. So following a pizza making course in Sorrento, Italy and finding a suitable vehicle, Hannah realised her father's dream to own a pizza truck.

Pizza Wagon is inspired by the pizza trucks Hannah and Zak encountered in Aix-en-Provence, France. And the wagon sure is a beauty! It's a vintage 1977 Citroen H Van that was originally used as a French farm vehicle, before being converted in the UK and shipped to Australia.

VERDE POMODORINI

MAKES 8 PIZZAS

PIZZA DOUGH

1 kg Italian 00 (pizza) flour
28 g sea salt, finely crushed
4 g yeast
700 ml cold water (you may use less than this)

HOMEMADE PESTO

1 large bunch basil
few parsley leaves
3 tablespoons parmesan cheese
2 tablespoons pine nuts
1 garlic clove, chopped
pinch of salt
extra virgin olive oil

PIZZA TOPPING

350 g (2⅓ cup) fior di latte (cow's milk mozzarella), torn into small pieces
32 cherry tomatoes, halved
120 g parmesan cheese, grated
extra virgin olive oil
16 slices prosciutto
1 small bunch fresh basil

It's best to make the pizza dough the day before. Tip the flour on to a clean work surface and make a well in the centre. Add the salt and yeast to the well then slowly start adding the water.

Using your fingers start bringing in the flour from the sides of the well, and mix the ingredients so that the water begins to thicken. Continue mixing the flour and water together until it forms a dough. Keep adding water until the dough is a nice soft consistency. If it's too dry add more water. If it's too sticky add more flour, until you get the desired result.

Knead the dough vigorously with light crisscross punches, for 15 minutes, to make a smooth and elastic dough. Cover with plastic wrap and leave in a warm place to rest for 15 minutes.

Remove the plastic wrap and knead the dough for another 5 minutes then divide the dough into approximately 200 g balls or 8 portions. Rub a small amount of olive oil over the surface of each ball. Place them into a lightly floured, sealed container and refrigerate for a minimum of 24 hours or a maximum of 72 hours. Leave plenty of space between each ball for it to rise and spread.

Make the pesto the next day. Combine all the ingredients (except the oil) in a food processor, and blend until well combined. Then, with the motor running, gradually add the oil in a thin, steady stream until combined.

Preheat a fan-forced oven to 250ºC (270ºC conventional/Gas 9).

Take one of the dough balls and, on a lightly floured surface, flatten the dough with your fingertips, turn it over and repeat. Rest the flattened dough on your knuckles and move the dough in a circular motion whilst stretching (watch out for fingernails!) and expanding it from the centre outwards, until you have an evenly stretched base.

Place the dough base on a pizza tray or pizza stone that has been lightly brushed with oil. Spread a thin layer of pesto over the base using a circular motion and leaving a couple of centimetres around the border pesto-free. Bake for 10 minutes.

Remove from the oven and scatter the fior di latte on the pizza, leaving lots of nice pesto gaps. Add about 8 cherry tomato halves, sprinkle with a generous amount of parmesan cheese and drizzle with olive oil. Bake for another 5 minutes.

Before serving top each pizza with plenty of fresh prosciutto and about 4 basil leaves. Eat immediately!

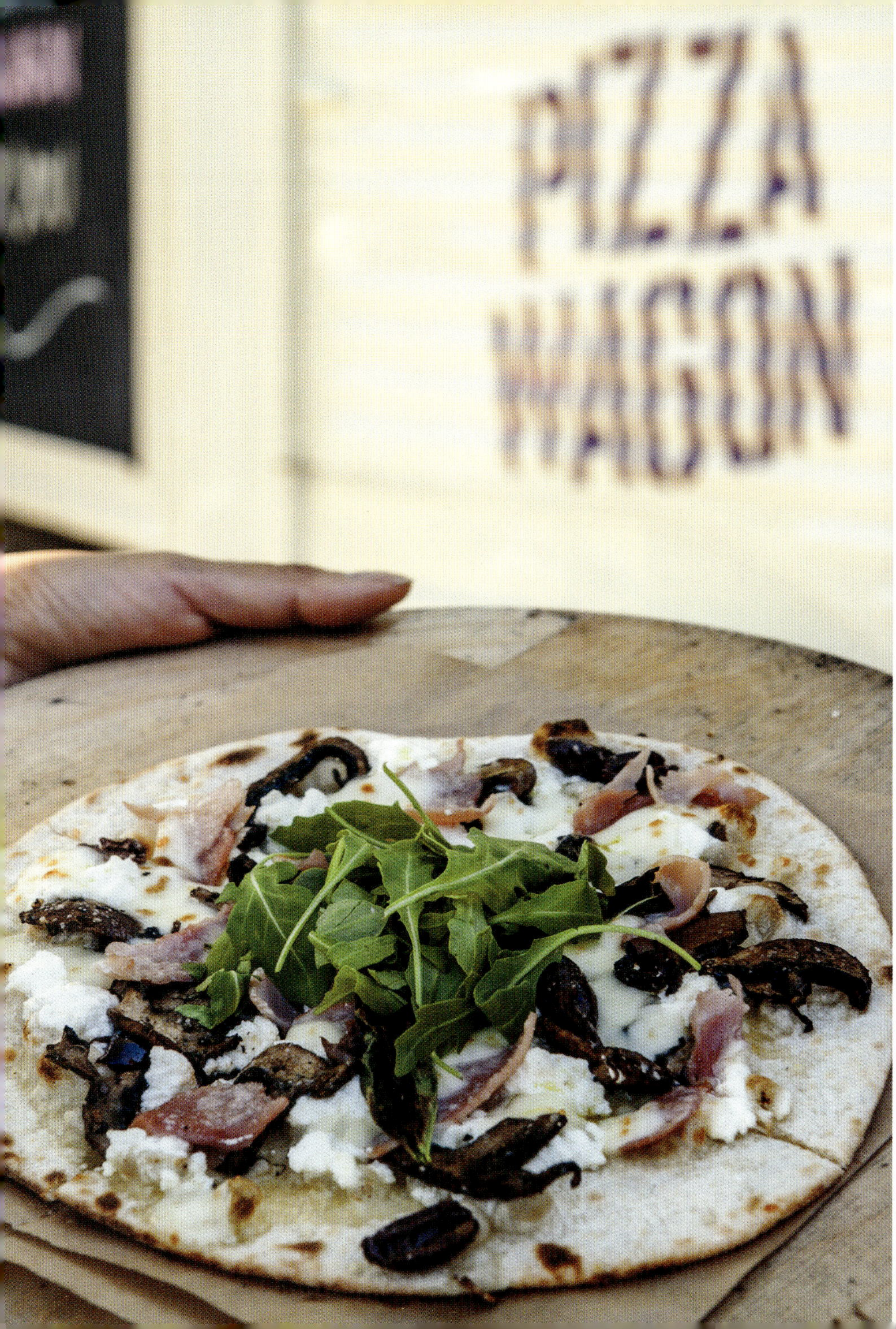
PIZZA
WAGON

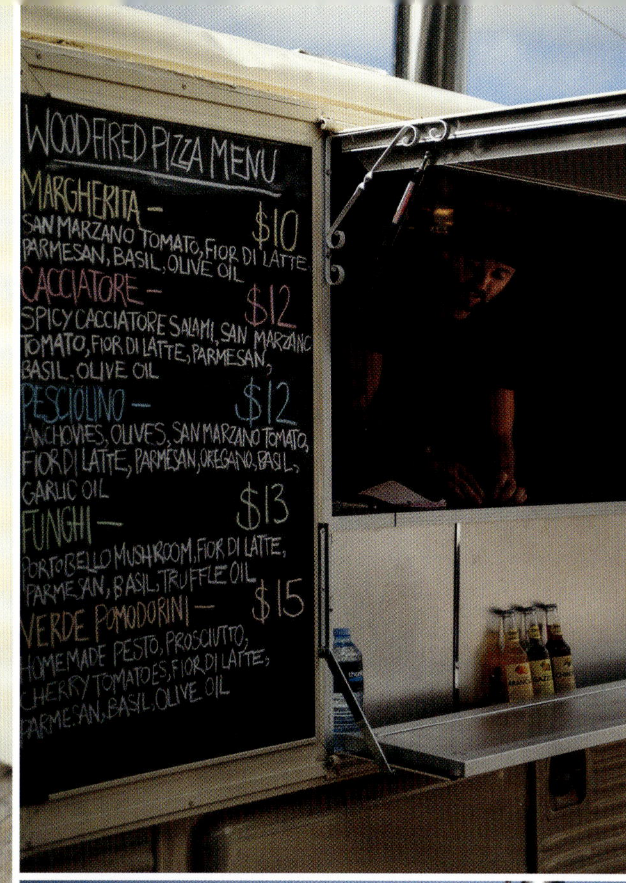

WOODFIRED PIZZA MENU
MARGHERITA – $10
SAN MARZANO TOMATO, FIOR DI LATTE
PARMESAN, BASIL, OLIVE OIL
CACCIATORE – $12
SPICY CACCIATORE SALAMI, SAN MARZANO
TOMATO, FIOR DI LATTE, PARMESAN,
BASIL, OLIVE OIL
PESCIOLINO – $12
ANCHOVIES, OLIVES, SAN MARZANO TOMATO,
FIOR DI LATTE, PARMESAN, OREGANO, BASIL,
GARLIC OIL
FUNGHI – $13
PORTOBELLO MUSHROOM, FIOR DI LATTE,
PARMESAN, BASIL, TRUFFLE OIL
VERDE POMODORINI – $15
HOMEMADE PESTO, PROSCIUTTO,
CHERRY TOMATOES, FIOR DI LATTE,
PARMESAN, BASIL, OLIVE OIL

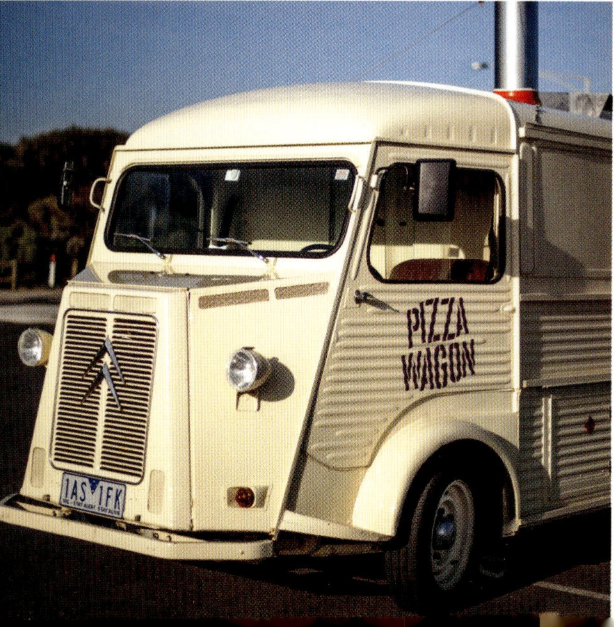

PIZZA
WAGON

WOODFIRED PIZZA
HANDMADE DOUGH
LOCAL, SEASONAL INGREDIENTS
YUMMY!
LURISA DRINKS — $3
LEMONADE, ORANGEADE, CHINOTTO
WATER — $2
WWW.PIZZAWAGON.COM.AU
FACEBOOK.COM/PIZZAWAGONMELB
INSTAGRAM @ PIZZAWAGONMELB
TWITTER @ PIZZAWAGONMELB
THANK YOU

WOODFIRED PIZZA MENU
MARGHERITA — $10
TOMATO, FIOR DI LATTE,
BASIL, OLIVE OIL
— $12
RE SAMNL SAN MARZANO
DI LATTE, PARMESAN,
OIL
— $12
ANCHOVIES, OLIVES, SAN MARZANO TOMATO,
FIOR DI LATTE, PARMESAN, OREGANO, BASIL,
GARLIC OIL
FUNGHI — $13
PORTOBELLO MUSHROOM, FIOR DI LATTE,
PARMESAN, BASIL, TRUFFLE OIL
VERDE POMODORINI — $15
HOMEMADE PESTO, PROSCIUTTO,
CHERRY TOMATOES, FIOR DI LATTE,
PARMESAN, BASIL, OLIVE OIL

PIZZA WAGON

PIZZA
WAGON

PIZZA
WAGON

pizzawagon.com.au

SOUL KITCHEN WOODFIRED PIZZA TRUCK

PERFECT PIZZA DOUGH

MAKES 6 PIZZAS

1 kg 00 (pizza) flour
600 ml purified or still mineral water*
2 g yeast
30 g Sicilian sea salt*

Place flour, water and yeast into a large mixing bowl. Mix together to form a dough. With clean hands, knead the dough well for 10–15 minutes, until smooth and elastic.

Add salt to the dough and knead until the salt is absorbed into the dough. Place the dough in a bowl and cover the bowl with plastic wrap and leave in a dark, cool space for 12–18 hours.

When the dough has almost doubled in size, divide it into approximately 250 g portions and roll into smooth balls. Place dough balls on a lightly floured tray. Leave the dough to rest for 30 minutes.

To use, flatten a dough ball with your fingertips and rolling pin to your desired size. Top with no more than four of your favourite toppings, and bake on a preheated pizza stone or thick terracotta tile at your oven's highest temperature for about 10 minutes, until the base is crispy.

**Using purified water is much better than tap water because yeast does not respond well with fluoride that is present in tap water.*

**Salt must be added at the end because salt can affect how well yeast works.*

Friends and business partners Michael and Paul are the men behind Soul Kitchen Woodfired Pizza Truck. Michael ran a mobile coffee cart in Melbourne, Australia for five years before getting together with Paul to expand his food offering. Although neither of them are Italian, both were keen to stay away from an already saturated burger/Mexican food market. So they bought a bus and worked towards installing a wood-fired oven that could heat up to 450ºC. Getting this gigantic, two-tonne oven to operate on a vehicle was quite an engineering feat and took a year to build.

Recently Michael and Paul have taken on a young pizza chef direct from Naples, with whom they are refining their wood-fired pizzas. Their pizzas are now cooked for only 90–120 seconds on a very high temperature (at least 350ºC) until there's a thin crust with the dough slightly bubbling. The final test is that you should be able to fold the pizza in half to eat it without the base cracking.

SOUL
KITCHEN

JULIETTE
ISABELLA
JULIETTE

SOUVLAKI CART

TZATZIKI (TALATTOURI)

SERVES 10–12

500 g (2 cups) creamy Greek-style yoghurt
175 g (1 cup) cucumber
1 teaspoon (approximately 3 cloves) garlic, finely crushed
1 teaspoon dried mint
1 tablespoon white wine vinegar (or lemon juice)
2 tablespoons extra virgin olive oil
salt and pepper

Place a sieve into a bowl and line with a tea towel. Scoop in the yoghurt and refrigerate for a few hours to allow excess liquid to drain through the sieve (this step will ensure you have a thick creamy tzatziki).

Grate the cucumber and squeeze out as much liquid as you can with your hands.

In a medium-size mixing bowl place the yoghurt, cucumber, garlic, mint, vinegar, olive oil, salt and pepper. Stir until thoroughly mixed. Serve with souvlaki, as a dip or as a side dish.

Kali Orexi (enjoy your meal!)

The idea for the Souvlaki Cart came to owner Ellen after her parents' olive grove and cafe fell victim to a bushfire in 2011. As her parents were not keen to rebuild this business, Ellen and her husband Shaun decided to put their teaching careers on hold, and take the opportunity to continue the family business, but in a slightly different way.

Encouraged by the growing number of food trucks in Melbourne, Australia the couple opted for a mobile food cart instead of another bricks-and-mortar business. They spent a good year converting a 1970s caravan into a functioning mobile kitchen, but then very quickly developed a solid business by first parking their van behind a supermarket.

Staying true to Ellen's Greek heritage, they serve souvlakis made with lamb, chicken or haloumi, based on recipes passed down from Ellen's mother and yiayia. They also offer a tasting plate, so you can try a bit of everything.

SOUVLAKI CART

COLOR RUNNER

souvlaki
CART

souvlaki
CART

URBAN PASTA

BOSCAIOLA SAUCE

SERVES 3–4

40 g unsalted butter
20 ml vegetable oil
½ garlic clove, finely chopped
150 g (1⅔ cups) Swiss brown mushrooms, diced
150 g shortcut bacon, diced
600 ml crème fraîche or pure cream
15 g (or ¼ bunch) spring onion, chopped

In a medium-size frying pan melt 20 g of the butter and the vegetable oil over medium heat. Once melted add the garlic and fry for 30 seconds before adding the diced mushrooms. Add a couple of pinches of salt and pepper. Cook the mushrooms for about 10 minutes (until cooked through) and set aside before they start sweating too much. Discard any liquid from the mushrooms.

In another medium-size frying pan, melt the remaining butter on high heat then add the bacon. Stir the bacon every minute or so until it is cooked (not crispy but it should be lightly browned).

Set the bacon aside but using the same frying pan (without washing it because all your flavours are there!) add the crème fraîche. Once the crème fraîche has warmed through return the bacon and mushrooms to the pan with a couple of pinches of salt (to your liking). Stir well and let it simmer until the crème fraîche starts to thicken.

Once the crème fraîche has thickened enough, add the spring onions, stir a little bit and your sauce is ready to be served on a bed of freshly cooked pasta.

Stephane, a young Frenchman from Paris came to Australia in 2005 to study computer science. Like many, he fell in love with a girl and the country, and literally kissed the City of Love goodbye in favour of a country of opportunity.

While working as a software engineer in Sydney, Australia, Stephane noticed that good pasta was only available from expensive up-market restaurants. He was convinced he could bring Sydneysiders fresh and reasonably priced pasta that's cooked to order, using simple and good-quality ingredients. Consulting a friend who happened to be a hand-making pasta expert, Stephane's plans would soon be realised.

Stephane stepped into his friend's commercial kitchen, where he learned the traditional art of pasta making, all while the Urban Pasta truck was being built. Two years on, Stephane is serving fresh pasta that's made especially for his truck, and using his own sauces. And while he may not be breaking any culinary boundaries, Stephane is doing exactly what he set out to do. With pasta including gnocchi, penne, ravioli and tortellini combined with sauces like arrabiata (spicy tomato), bolognese or lamb ragout, Urban Pasta followers never have to worry about ordering the same dish twice – unless they want to, of course.

URBAN
PASTA

URBAN PASTA
URBAN
PASTA
HUNGRY?
DETOUR
NO LIMIT
STOP

URBAN
PASTA

URBAN
PASTA

URBANPASTA

URBAN
PASTA
DONE
GROW
MAKE IT
SOON

with South American & Mexican amigos

AL CARBON

For many, the motivation for starting a food truck business is simple. It's seen as a cheaper and possibly easier way to test out a food venture. For Al Carbon owner Attila, the motivation to open up a food truck business was less conventional. Having worked as an undercover policeman in Sydney, Australia for many years, Attila encountered many brutal cases. One case that really affected him left Attila diagnosed with post-traumatic stress disorder, and he was honourably discharged from the force.

Attila travelled to Mexico and LA to research Mexican cuisine, 'downing' 30 tacos a day. Two years later his buzzing food truck business brings new meaning to the expression, 'Let food be thy medicine'!

Apart from a range of tacos, Al Carbon also serves nachos and beans with chiltepil, a dry salsa made with chilli, sesame and pumpkin seeds. The sanchos are also delicious.

SANCHOS

Bacon-wrapped, cheese–stuffed jalapeño peppers with avocado and tomatillo salsa

MAKES 4

AVOCADO SALSA

2 avocados
1 lime, juiced
5 medium tomatillos* (from the tin)
1 garlic clove
½ white onion
1 jalapeño, seeded and veins removed to reduce the heat

JALAPEÑOS

4 medium-size jalapeños
4 garlic cloves, crushed
4 pinches of Mexican oregano
4 tablespoons oaxacan cheese*
8 strips streaky smoked bacon, sliced slightly thicker than prosciutto

To make the avocado salsa, place all the ingredients (keep the juice of the tomatillos aside) into a food processor or blender and pulse to create a smooth paste. Add the juice of the tomatillos to create a smooth creamy salsa.

Rub the inside of the jalapeños with the garlic cloves and sprinkle with the Mexican oregano. Stuff the jalapeños with the cheese then wrap the outside with two pieces of streaky bacon each. Press the pieces of bacon together to help them hold in place.

You can also use a small bamboo skewer, pre-soaked in water, to hold the jalapeño together. This also makes it easier to flip them when cooking.

Grill the jalapeño over charcoal or on a hot plate until the cheese has melted and the chilli starts to blister.

Serve in a tortilla or with corn chips topped with the avocado salsa.

Note: have some labne or Greek yoghurt on standby to alleviate the heat.

** Tomatillos are available from specialty food stores.*

** Oaxacan cheese is available from specialty food stores. Alternatively you can use Lebanese haloumi, washed and soaked in water for 1 hour to reduce the saltiness.*

GUACATE
DE AL CARBÓN

Al Carbón
@AlCarbón'a
Visit Al Carbón
Visit Al Carbón.m

VISIT AL CARBÓN
Visit Al Carbon

VISIT BEAUTIFUL
AL CARB
DIRECCIÓN GENERAL DE TURIS
AV. JUAREZ 89
AL CARB
X·7
NEW SO
Al Carbón

CANTINA MOVIL

AUTENTICO PINTO BEANS

SERVES 4

200 g (1 cup) dried pinto beans
½ teaspoon dried Mexican oregano
1 fresh bay leaf
1 tablespoon olive oil
1 onion, finely chopped
1 red capsicum, seeded and membranes removed, finely chopped
2 garlic cloves, crushed
1½ teaspoon smoked paprika
1 teaspoon ground cumin
400 g tinned crushed tomatoes
1 tablespoon fresh oregano leaves, finely chopped

Begin this recipe a day ahead. Place the pinto beans in a bowl and cover with cold water. Cover and leave to soak overnight on a bench.

The next day, rinse the beans, place them in a small pot and cover with fresh cold water. Bring to the boil, then drain and rinse once more. Refresh the pot with cold water to 1 cm above the beans, add the dried oregano and fresh bay leaf and simmer for 25–35 minutes, until tender and cooked. Drain the beans, keeping the water in reserve.

Heat the oil in a large saucepan over medium heat. Add the onion and capsicum, and cook, stirring, for 6–8 minutes, until softened. Add the garlic and cook, stirring, for 30 seconds, then add the paprika and cumin and continue stirring. Cook for 1 minute, then add the tomato and fresh oregano leaves and season to taste. Simmer for 5–6 minutes, then remove from the heat.

Add the beans to the tomato mixture, along with 80 ml (⅓ cup) reserved water from the beans. Return to heat and bring to the boil then remove from heat and season to taste.

Serve in tacos, burritos or nachos.

Australia is so culturally diverse that no-one is likely to question the fact that Cantina Movil, a Mexican food truck in Sydney, is owned by Stephanie who's half-Australian and half-Italian, and her husband Rody who's half-Maltese and half-German.

After operating a bar in Sydney's Manly area for nine years, selling Mexican food from a truck was a relatively easy transition for this couple. They recently added a second truck to their fleet, sporting a fancy-ass hydraulic roof, which flips up to reveal a kind of open-air kitchen. Rody designed the roof mechanism himself to allow the truck to fit into smaller spaces when the roof is closed.

Festival-goers and city workers eagerly await their weekly hit of burritos, soft-shell tacos and nachos. If you prefer, you can also have your burrito naked – without the tortilla, that is!

ORDER HERE

please
ORDER AT TRUCK

CERVEZA·AGUILA
Cerveceria de Colombia

CHIMICHURRI GRILL

At age 15, Chimichurri Grill owner Greg took a job washing dishes for Gaucho's in Adelaide, which claims to be Australia's first Argentinean restaurant. He must have been doing something right, because within two years he was promoted to cook and operated the grill there. Little did he realise then that this was to play a big part later in his life.

Greg then spent time overseas, taking different jobs including teaching English in Japan and working for a carbon trading company, but starting a family brought him back to Australia. He bought a camper trailer and travelled around Australia with his family for two years. At the end of their trip, the family moved back to Adelaide where Greg struggled to find work. This is how the idea of an Argentinean food truck slowly came to the fore.

Chimichurri Grill serves a typical Argentinean choripán sandwich filled with chorizo, roasted capsicum, rocket, mayonnaise, provolone cheese and homemade chimichurri sauce. There are also some other combinations filled with steak, chicken or a slice of grilled provolone for the vegetarians. Chunky, hand-cut chips and Greg's signature 'chimi mayo' dipping sauce are the only accompaniments to this relatively small menu. But if you do what you do well, who needs more?

CHIMI STEAK ROLL

SERVES 1

150 g scotch fillet steak
1 fresh ciabatta roll
Kewpie mayonnaise*
handful of fresh rocket leaves
10–15 g provolone piccante cheese, grated

CHIMICHURRI SAUCE

½ teaspoon smoked paprika
½ teaspoon sweet paprika
1 teaspoon ground fennel
1 small bunch flat-leaf parsley
3 garlic cloves, peeled
100 ml red wine vinegar
20 ml fresh lemon juice
1 teaspoon dijon mustard
salt
pepper
300 ml pure vegetable oil

For the best results, cook the steak using the sous-vide method. Put the steak in a standard zip-lock bag or use a vacuum food sealer, and place in water in a sous-vide cooker or pot. Cook for approximately 100 minutes (1 hour and 40 minutes) at 58.9ºC; if cooking in a pot, use a thermometer to check the water temperature.

Otherwise, simply place the raw steak on a hot chargrill plate, cook the slices of steak for 1 minute on each side. If cooking from raw, more cooking time may be required.

To make the chimichurri sauce, blend all the ingredients in a blender, except the oil. Once the ingredients are fully combined, continue to blend while gradually adding the oil in a slow, steady stream to prevent the mixture from splitting.

Cut the ciabatta roll in half, spread with a layer of mayonnaise, add the rocket leaves and a sprinkle of grated provolone cheese. Drizzle with chimichurri sauce and place the steak on top. Add a little more chimichurri sauce to taste.

** Kewpie mayonnaise is a brand of Japanese mayonnaise and is available in the Asian foods aisle of supermarkets.*

CHIMICHURRI
Grill

Mobile Gourmet Argentinian Food
CHIMICHURRI
Grill

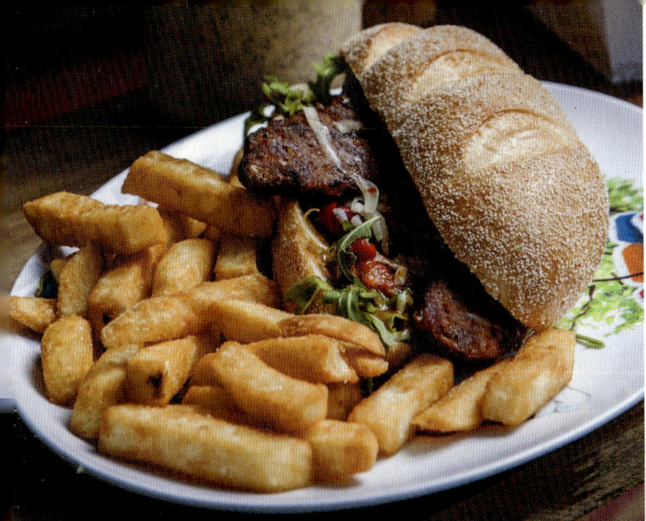

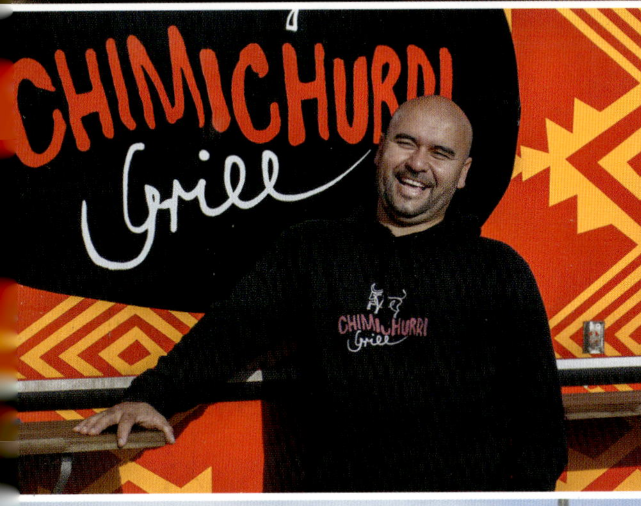

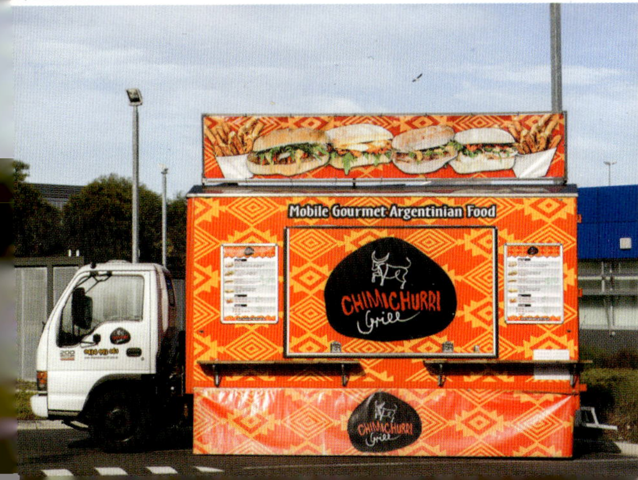

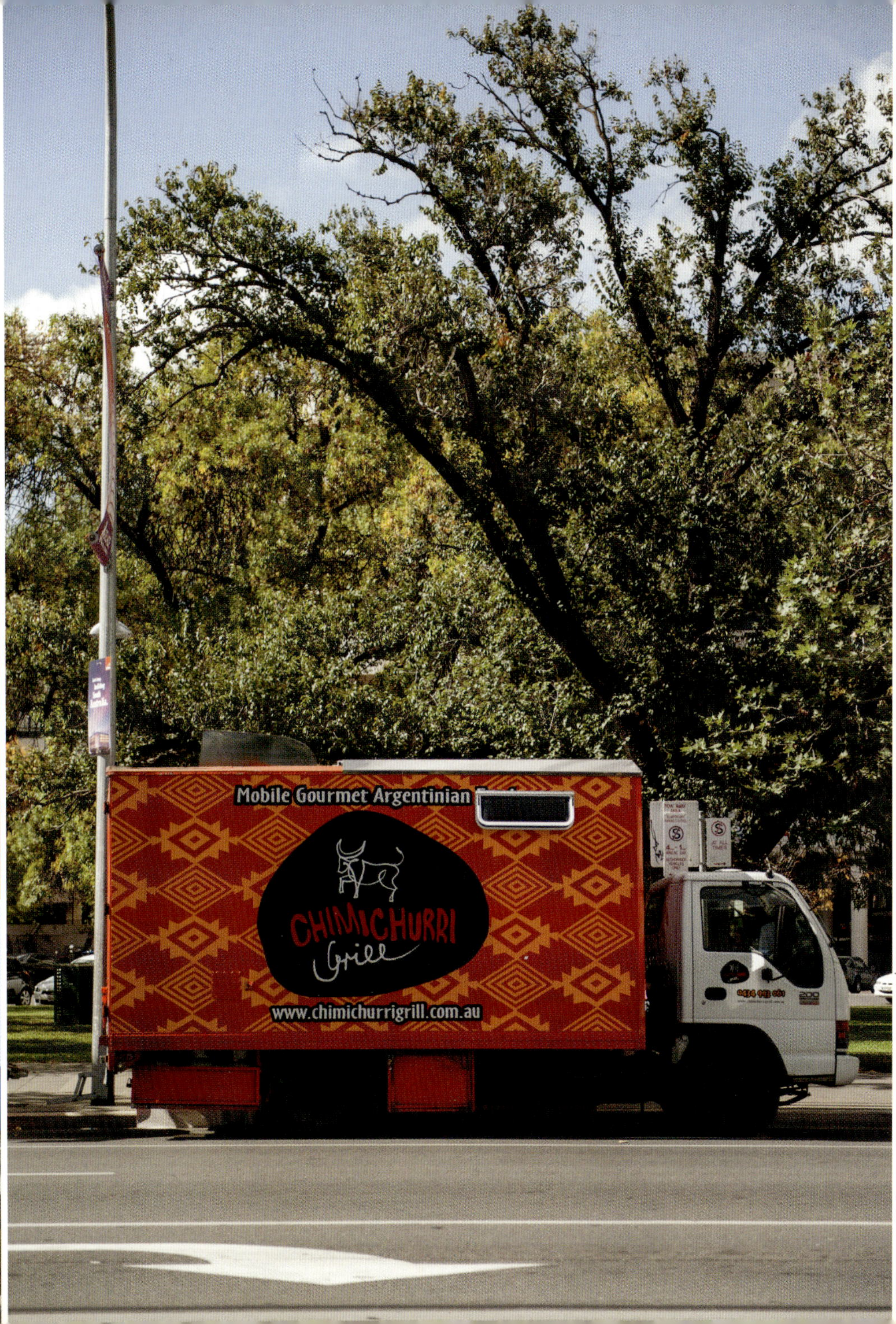
Mobile Gourmet Argentinian
CHIMICHURRI
Grill
www.chimichurrigrill.com.au

CHINGÓN TACO TRUCK

Chingón, the Mexican slang word meaning all things cool, is the bad-ass brainchild of hermanos (brothers) Mick and Will, who grew up just south of Alberquerque, New Mexico. Living so close to the Mexican border, many of the flavours, decor and music of their Mexican neighbours were practically in their backyard.

Fitted out by the brothers themselves, Chingón's ultra-cool, copper-plated trailer is nicknamed 'La Llorona', or weeping woman, after a legend of a beautiful woman whose restless soul is said to haunt the rivers with her weeping. After having been rejected by her lover, she drowns her children in a jealous fit and then regretting her horrible act,

drowns herself. The story stuck with Mick and Will through their childhood, as their mother would warn them not to play in ditches or else 'La Llorona' would get them.

But Chingón's ultimate Mexican street-food menu will only give you good reasons to weep. There's elote en vaso (a hotted-up cup of fresh corn kernels with cheese), and tacos made with the boys' very own blue-corn tortillas and not-so-standard fillings like achiote pulled pork and grilled pineapple, charcoal steak with black beans, and grilled fish with lime and chipotle crema. Also on the menu are tamales, and a grilled chicken and tortilla soup.

ELOTE EN VASO

Chargrilled corn in a cup

SERVES 8

CHIPOTLE CREMA

500 g (2 cups) sour cream
2 tablespoons fresh coriander, finely chopped
25 ml fresh lime juice
45 g (¼ cup) brown sugar
1 teaspoon chipotle powder* (it is essential that chipotle is used)

CORN BASE

8–10 ears of sweet yellow corn, shucked (tinned corn can be used but is not recommended)
75 g unsalted butter, melted
1 teaspoon salt
¼ lime, juiced
queso fresco*
pinch of chipotle powder*

To make the chipotle crema, hand whisk the sour cream, coriander, lime juice, brown sugar and chipotle powder together in a medium-size bowl, until thick and creamy.

To prepare the corn base, cook the corn on a chargrill until slightly blackened. Remove the kernels from the grill and boil them in a pot for 15 minutes. Stir in the melted butter and salt. Set the corn mixture aside and keep warm.

Spoon enough corn mixture to half-fill a 300 ml paper cup. Pour the lime juice over the corn. Top with the chipotle crema and crumbed queso fresco. Sprinkle the chipotle powder over the top.

It is important to give the dish a good mix in the cup to blend all the flavours together before eating (avoids a mouth full of cheese on the first bite). The dish only comes together properly when the corn, the lime, the chipotle crema and the cheese all work in unison.

** Chipotle powder is available from specialty food stores.*

** Queso fresco is available from specialty food stores, or you can use a crumbly feta).*

EST 2013
CHINGÓN
TACOS

CHINGÓN
TACOS

COMIDA DO SUL

COMIDA *PRATO FEITO*

In Brazil the prato feito *(often abbreviated to PF on menus and signboards in Brazil) is a popular choice for lunch because it is a cheap and hearty meal. The literal translation of* prato feito *is 'composed plate', because it includes a protein (beef, chicken, fish), beans, rice, French fries (Comida use cassava chips instead) and vinaigrette salad.*

If you want to use a picanha (a popular cut of beef for this dish) ask your butcher for the 'rump cap'; it is a triangular cut with fat on top.

Every Brazilian has their own family recipe. The flavours are so simple, however, that you can add a few other favourite spices to create your own version.

SERVES 15

BLACK BEANS
750 g dried black beans (we use black turtle
    beans)
3 litres water
3–4 small bay leaves
5 garlic cloves, finely chopped
1 onion, chopped
½ tablespoon sweet paprika
½ tablespoon salt

MEAT
1 kg meat (your choice of protein)
Forofa*

RICE
3 cups long-grain white rice, uncooked
6 cups water
4 garlic cloves, crushed
½ brown onion, diced
water to cover rice

GARLICKY KALE
1 large bunch kale, finely shredded
60 ml (¼ cup) olive oil
4 garlic cloves, crushed
salt

VINAIGRETTE
5 tomatoes
1 red onion
dash of red wine vinegar
olive oil
salt

To make the black beans, rinse them well in a colander, then place them in a 6 litre pressure cooker. Pour 3 litres of water into the pressure cooker and cook for 40 minutes. Turn the heat off and release the pressure through the secure valve. Do not open until all the pressure is released; check your pressure cooker manual for other security checks. If you don't have a pressure cooker you can soak the beans overnight in the of water.

Place the soaked beans in a pot with the water from the pressure cooker and cook for about 1 hour on medium heat, until the beans become soft. If some foam forms while cooking the beans, just remove it with a spoon.

When the beans are cooked, add the bay leaves and keep on medium heat, stirring occasionally for at least 2 hours, until the beans are mushy.

In a frying pan heat some olive oil and fry the garlic. Then add the onion. Cook until the onions are soft.

Add the onion preparation to the beans, along with the paprika. Then add the salt, adding more until you achieve the desired taste. Add pepper to your liking.

To thicken the beans mixture crush some of the beans at the bottom of the pot with your spoon and then stir through; if it doesn't have much juice add a bit of water and bring to the boil.

Using your choice of meat, cook it on a frying pan to your liking. If using picanha beef, trim the fat to about 1 cm thick and place on a hot frying pan or grill. Sear all of the surfaces of the meat, cooking the fat side last. Remove the whole rump from the frying pan and cut the rump into large steaks. Salt the steaks and return them to the frypan or grill, and cook to your liking.

Once cooked, let the steaks rest for a few minutes then slice into small 1 cm long pieces. Roll the meat in the farofa before eating!

For the boiled rice, put the rice into a large pot with the water and bring to the boil. Reduce the heat, add the garlic and onion and simmer with the lid on for 20 minutes, or until the water has been completely absorbed. Remove the pot from the heat and leave covered for 5 minutes. Fluff the rice with a fork before serving.

To make the garlicky kale, fry the kale in a frying pan with the olive oil, garlic and a bit of salt. Cook for 2 minutes.

For the vinaigrette salad, chop the tomatoes and the red onion. Mix them with the red wine vinegar, olive oil and salt.

Serve the beans, meat, garlicky kale and vinaigrette salad on the rice.

**Forofa is a toasted manioc flour mixture with a smoky, salty taste used to accentuate the flavour of meat. It can be found in specialty food stores.*

Having dabbled in photography and film, food truck owner Joel accompanied a film producer for a four-day whirlwind tour of Sao Paolo, Brazil. Surprisingly, four days was enough time for Joel to fall in love with both the city and a girl named Dani. Returning to see if the love affair was something more serious, he spent another two months in Brazil and fell deeper in love, not just with the girl, but also with Brazil's lively culture, music and food.

Moving to Perth, Australia for a shared life together, Joel and Dani were keen to bring over the flavours and cultural spirit of Brazil. And as the food truck scene was just starting out in Perth, they thought a Brazilian food truck would be a good vehicle (pun intended). Operating since 2013, Comida do Sul serves authentic Brazilian dishes with recipes that Dani had been taught by her mother and grandmother. Their menu includes coxinha, a teardrop-shaped croquette made of mashed potato with a meat centre. True to Brazilian tradition, their signature dish is prato feito (see below), but they also sell batata frita (shoestring fries), choripán (an Argentinean-style hotdog filled with chorizo) and fresh coconut water.

CORNUTOPIA

ESQUITES

Mexican corn salad

SERVES 4 AS A SIDE DISH

2 tablespoons vegetable oil
600 g (3 cups) corn (about 4 ears), cut from the cob
1 jalapeño, seeded and finely diced
3 tablespoons sour cream
1 lime, juiced
3 spring onions, sliced
1 handful fresh coriander, chopped
1 garlic clove, grated
2 tablespoons cotija* (or feta), crumbled
chilli powder to taste

coriander leaves (additional) and a wedge of lime to garnish

Pour the oil on a grill or into a heavy skillet over medium–high heat. Add the corn kernels and cook until charred, then toss the corn to mix in the grill or skillet and let it char again. This will take 5–10 minutes depending on your grill heat and the size of the corn kernels. Add the jalapeño and sauté for a minute then remove from heat.

Place all other ingredients in a medium-size bowl. Add the corn mixture to it and stir.

Garnish with coriander and a wedge of lime.

**Cotija can be purchased from specialty food stores.*

Corn. Who doesn't love to get their teeth into the sweet, golden, crunchy stuff? Which makes Cornutopia a big, bright-yellow celebration of this staple ingredient for many parts of the world.

With an all-girl, all-capable crew behind her, Cornutopia's '60s converted caravan came to life after Ellie's overseas travels in countries where corn is the hero of many meals. Ellie's first career was in the rag trade, working for labels such as Queen. But her switch from rags to food is best explained in her own words, in that 'it's easier to sell 20 tacos than a $200 dress'.

Cornutopia uses local, organic and free-range produce as much as possible to serve up delicious, authentic Mexican treats such as soft-shell tacos, burritos and quesadillas.

And you'd never know it, but the precise shade of yellow on her caravan is the same as that for local taxis (which was a much cheaper paint option!).

Cornutopia
CORNUTOPIA.COM.AU
FRESH NOT FANCY  
TACOS and Sweet Potato 
Cornutopia

TACOS AND Sweet Corn

FLAVOUR FIESTA: with South American & Mexican amigos

DOS DIABLOS MOBILE CANTINA

PICO DE GALLO SALSA

Pico de gallo salsa is really easy to prepare fresh. This uncooked salsa is also known throughout Mexico as salsa fresca or salsa Mexicana. In the truck they use it with their carnitas tacos because the fresh, zesty flavours cut nicely through the richness of the meat, however it goes really well with just about anything. Bill loves it as a dip with corn tortilla chips or with any kind of eggs. It's also a salsa that lends itself to lots of personal variations; feel free to play around with the quantities to adjust them to your personal taste, or add extras such as garlic or even avocado. As Dinosaur Jr said, 'Start choppin'!'

6 medium tomatoes, diced
2 white (or Spanish) onions, finely chopped
1 large bunch fresh coriander, finely chopped
2 jalapeños, seeded and finely chopped (optional)

Combine and stir all ingredients in a large bowl, until evenly mixed, adding lime juice and salt to taste. Cover and refrigerate for 30 minutes.

Watch out for the big red truck. If you see it, don't step aside. In fact, make an immediate beeline for it. The red Dos Diablos Mobile Cantina used to be a fire fighters' canteen truck, but these days it's only fiery thanks to the chilli sauces that accompany owner Bill's concise but popular menu. Bill offers exactly three types of tacos – 'carnitas', slow-roasted pork served with pico de gallo sauce; 'pollo', marinated and grilled chicken that comes with corn salsa and chipotle mayonnaise; and 'vego', which comes with black beans and salsa verde.

Self-proclaimed devil-in-chief Bill witnessed the rise of food trucks in Mexico and the States, and quickly realised how well they would work in Australia. According to Bill, 'Australia is quite an irreverent, informal culture, so the idea of being able to grab a six pack [of beers] or bottle of wine, head down to the park or beach and enjoy some quality food with friends just seems such an ideal fit.'

The truck enjoyed its 15 minutes of fame when it was used in a TV commercial for a major Australian bank, requiring Bill to drive down a major highway accompanied by a six-car police entourage for safety. Now that's true rockstar treatment!

IV'S BURRITOS

SMOKEY BARBECUE PULLED PORK

SERVES 6–8

1–1.5 kg pork shoulder, de-boned and skin on (look for pork with thick fat layer under skin)

BARBECUE SAUCE
190 ml (¾ cup) tomato sauce
190 ml (¾ cup) water
60 ml (¼ cup) apple cider vinegar
1 teaspoon salt
¼ teaspoon freshly ground pepper
1 teaspoon smoked paprika
1 teaspoon ground mustard
½ teaspoon ground cumin
1½ tablespoons worcestershire sauce
1 teaspoon blended chipotles in adobo sauce* (otherwise just enough chilli powder for mild background heat, approximately ½ teaspoon)
1 tablespoon brown sugar
1 teaspoon liquid smoke*
2 garlic cloves, crushed

crusty bread and lime juice and wedges to serve

Preheat a fan-forced oven to 100ºC (120ºC convential/Gas 1). Place the unseasoned pork shoulder, skin side up, in a large high-sided roasting tray and cook at 100ºC in a fan-forced oven (lowest temperature in a convential oven, Gas 1) for 10–12 hours, until the meat is falling apart. Ensure there is enough room around the pork in the tray so that it doesn't stew.

Fifteen minutes before taking the pork out of the oven combine all the barbecue sauce ingredients in a saucepan, bring to the boil and simmer for 5 minutes. Set aside.

Once the pork is done, remove the skin and excess fat, and with two forks pull the meat apart into small pieces. Place the pork into the barbecue sauce and stir gently, too much stirring will make the pork lose texture.

Spoon onto crusty bread and serve with lime wedges.

**Chipotles in adobo sauce and liquid smoke can be found at specialty food stores.*

Iv's Burritos food truck owner Ivan left a career in accounting at the age of 24 after only one year in the job. You could assume that he just wasn't into it, but in fact, after working for a company that sells software for small home businesses, Ivan may have learnt enough to realise that he too could start up his own small business.

Like many, Ivan's travels in the US and Mexico inspired his own Mexican food truck. And although he has no formal hospitality training, Ivan has always been a passionate cook and practised his burritos on his friends before committing to buying his trailer. Iv's Burritos currently offers just two main fillings: smoky barbecue pulled pork or Mexican grilled chicken. Add to this oregano-infused rice, salsa and hot sauce, and no amigo is left hungry.

iv's burritos
ivsburritos.com.au

iv's burr
ivsburritos.com

JUAN MORE TACO

SENCILLO HORCHATA

MAKES 2 LITRES (8 CUPS)

150 g (¾ cup) white long-grain rice, uncooked
1 cinnamon stick
375 ml carnation milk
150 g (⅔ cup) caster sugar
1 teaspoon vanilla extract

cinnamon powder, for dusting

In a medium-size bowl place the rice and cinnamon stick and cover with water, allow to sit for 30 minutes.

Transfer to a blender and whizz until smooth. Strain the liquid through a very fine sieve or strainer covered with muslin cloth. If the liquid is fairly gritty you might need to repeat the straining process again.

Pour the strained liquid into a 2-litre serving jug. Add the sugar and stir until combined. Add the carnation milk, vanilla extract and enough water to bring the total volume to 2 litres.

To serve, pour the liquid over ice and dust with some cinnamon powder.

The name of this food truck began as joke when owner Naomi found this gorgeous 1960s vintage bus, which was originally used to sell doughnuts. The interior needed to be completely re-fitted, but Naomi decided to keep as much of its exterior features as possible to maintain its original character.

It's hats (or sombreros) off to Naomi who, after a long career in nursing, has found the inspiration and energy to try out a completely new career in running a Mexican food truck. Her love for Mexican food developed during holidays in LA and Mexico, where she actively sought out food tours and taco classes to learn the fine art and craft of Mexican street food.

Juan More Taco's menu includes elote en vaso (corn in a cup) and tacos (called 'Juans') of almost every persuasion. So you can have a pork Juan, a chicken Juan or a beef Juan … or you can even get a veggie Juan or two. To wash it all down there's a choice of agua de horchata (a Mexican rice-milk drink) or agua de Jamaica (cold hibiscus tea).

With business booming, Naomi is also looking to ensure the long-term future of her food truck. She's actively building a community of food trucks in Brisbane, Australia by organising regular food truck festivals under the quirky name, Phenomnomnom.

JUAN
MORE
TACO
TACO61

ACO

www.juanmoretaco.com.au
Follow Us · JuanMoreTacoBus
JUAN
MORE
TACO

JUAN
MORE
TACO
QLD TACO61
CORONA EXTRA

LA CANTINA CO

SESAME-CRUSTED TUNA TACO

MAKES 6 TACOS

CREAMY HOT SAUCE
2 teaspoons habanero-based hot sauce
4 teaspoons sour cream
2 teaspoons fresh coriander, roughly chopped

GUACAMOLE
1 large avocado
150 g pico de gallo*
salt and pepper
½ lime, juiced

150 g sesame seeds, semi-crushed (with a spice grinder
    or mortar and pestle)
2 pinches of sea salt flakes
2 pinches of freshly cracked pepper
400 g tuna fillet, sliced into 12.5 cm (5 inch) long slices
6 × 6 inch soft-shell taco (wheat-based preferred)
half red cabbage, sliced into long thin fingers
fresh coriander, to garnish

Make the creamy hot sauce by mixing the habanero sauce with
the sour cream and the coriander in a small bowl, until silky
and creamy.

To make the guacamole, mash the avocado with the pico
de gallo, salt, pepper and lime juice.

Mix the semi-crushed sesame seeds, sea salt flakes and
freshly cracked pepper in a medium-size bowl. Coat the tuna
in the sesame seed mix, then shallow fry the tuna in hot pan
for 3–4 minutes, until golden brown/slightly blackened (but
not burnt).

In another pan, without oil or with very little oil, crisp up a taco
until golden brown and puffy on both sides.

Place some tuna on the crispy taco, then layer with red cabbage,
guacamole and creamy hot sauce, and garnish with some
fresh coriander.

** Pico de gallo is available from specialty food stores.*

When the original owner of La Cantina Co put his business up for sale, university student Anton thought quickly and got together with brothers Sam and Jake, suggesting that between the three of them they could make a go of running this Mexican cantina. About nine months into their own venture, they seem to be doing a damn fine job with it.

The three of them clearly share a brave entrepreneurial spirit, as they've still got their university degrees to complete; Anton is studying winemaking and commercial accounting; Jake is studying nutrition and personal fitness; and Sam has economics covered. Defying the stereotypes of being laid-back Gen Ys, these boys work hard to balance their studies as well as operate a successful food truck in a competitive environment.

Anton travels to the US regularly, as his parents live in California. There he has seen the long-term potential of food trucks and has ambitions to perhaps one day serve food in retail outlets or to open up a bar or cafe. Refining the La Cantina Co menu since the previous owner's version, the boys serve tacos, quesadillas and burritos with a variety of fillings. They hand you a meal in such a friendly, laid-back style, no-one would guess that they were balancing university studies at the same time.

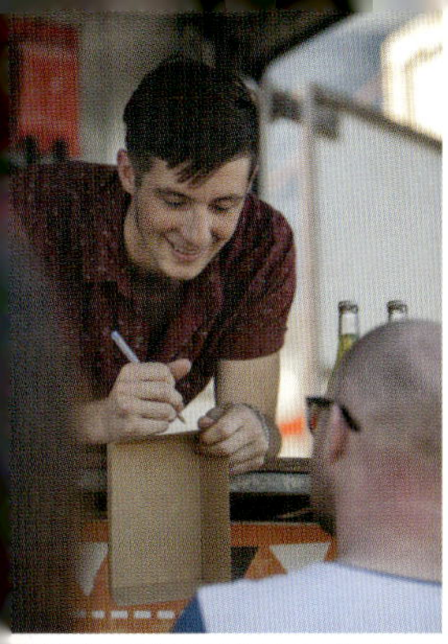

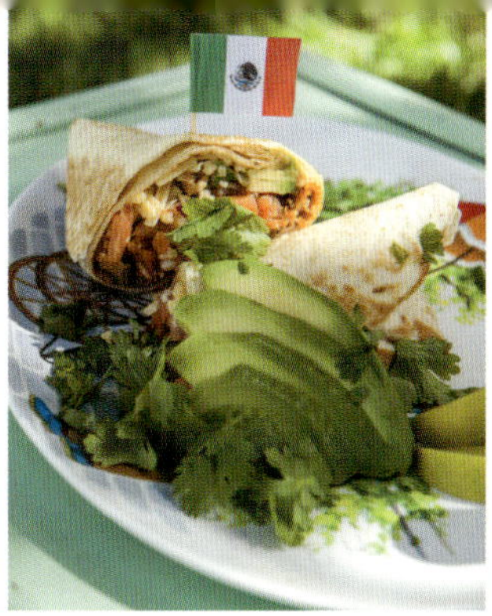

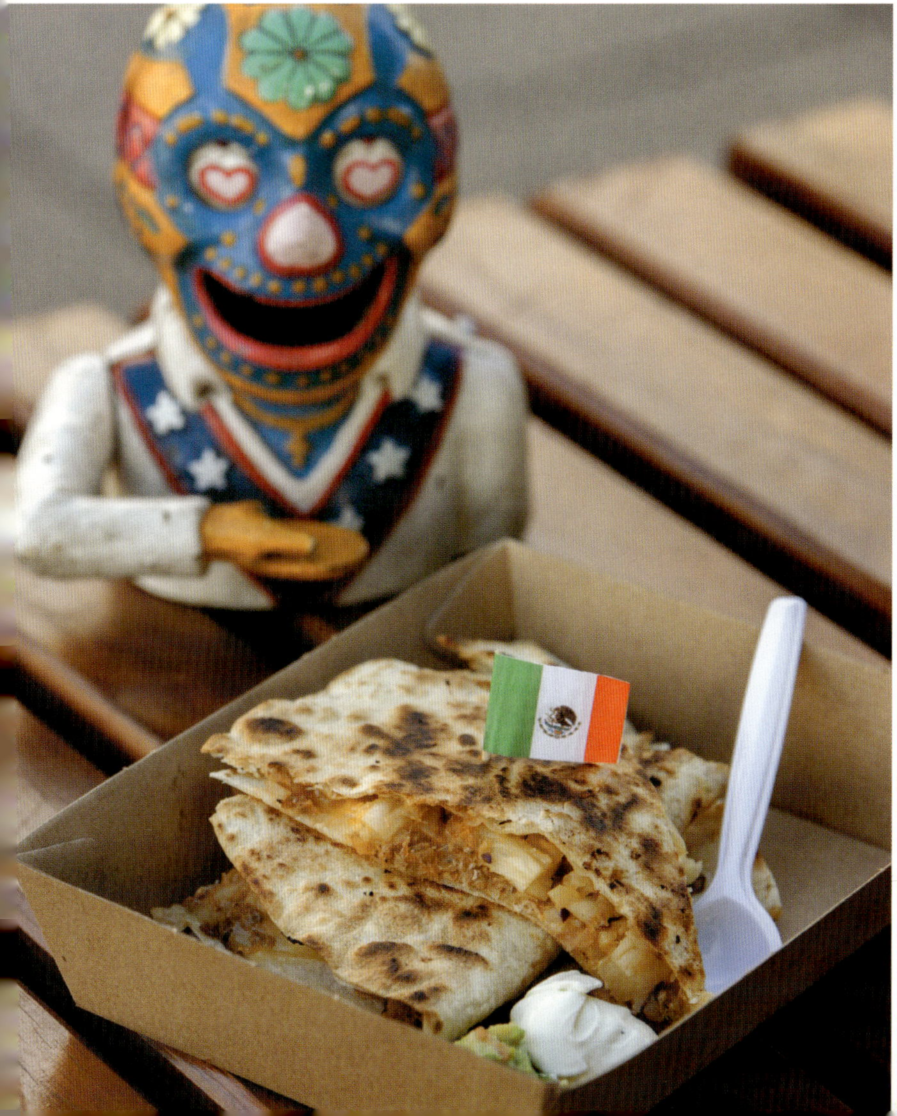

LA CHIVA

GUASACACA DIPPING SAUCE

This punchy sauce, originally from Venezuela, is like a party for your taste buds. Guasacaca can also be used as a marinade for fish, chicken or red meat.

Tapioca crisps are a popular accompaniment to guasacaca dipping sauce. Made from the cassava root and similar to sweet potato, tapioca is the most popular chip ingredient in the tropical parts of South America.

2 bunches fresh coriander
1 small green capsicum, seeded
2 garlic cloves, peeled
½ brown onion, chopped
1 teaspoon white vinegar
pinch of ground black pepper
pinch of sea salt
1 tablespoon olive oil

tapioca chips, to serve

Clean the coriander roots very well, getting rid of any dry ends, then roughly chop the whole coriander: the roots, stems and leaves.

Put the chopped coriander, capsicum, garlic, onion and all remaining ingredients in a blender, and blend at low speed until a paste forms.

Serve as a dipping sauce with tapioca chips.

Chiva is a Spanish word meaning goat. But according to owner Freddy who hails from Colombia, chiva is also an endearing nickname for the rickety, old buses that travel the narrow and curvy roads in Colombia's countryside and mountain ranges. Most of the time they are overcrowded with people, produce and even farm animals. In other words, the ride is lively and somewhat crazy.

Having immigrated to Adelaide, Australia to be with his Australian wife, Freddy set up his La Chiva food truck business to capture the South American flavours and cultural vibrancy he's grown up with. These days a chiva is also known as a type of party bus that has gained popularity in the States, transporting party people between bars and clubs with Latin music blasting out of it. Freddy may not be transporting people around physically, but with his South American–inspired menu featuring tapioca chips, chorizo burgers and Amazonian rice (and funky grooves pumping out of his converted bus), he's certainly transporting the flavours and feel of his home country to Adelaide.

PICK UP
laChiva
SOUTH AMERICAN FLAVOURS

OI! TACO

Oi! Taco owners and friends Chantal and Clare met while working for a public art construction company. Tired of working in a male-dominated industry with politics and bureaucracy to contend with, the two decided to literally put their money where the mouths are and bring their mutual love for Mexican street food to Brisbane, Australia.

Relying on their combined expertise in marketing strategy and accounting, they tested out their food at markets and festivals before purchasing 'Lupe', their endearingly named trailer. It came ready-made with a mural painted by a local artist about which they have mixed feelings (the mural, that is).

Mexican food may be popular, but Chantal and Clare take it up a notch and make their own tortillas every day. Along with such standards as soft-shell tacos and quesadillas, Oi! Taco also offers home-style breakfasts like huevos rancheros, chorizo scramble and their own homemade hibiscus tea.

SLOW-COOKED SKIRT STEAK

MAKES APPROXIMATELY 20–30 TORTILLAS

2 tablespoons smoked paprika
1 teaspoon onion powder
1 teaspoon garlic powder
1 teaspoon ground mustard
1 teaspoon sweet paprika
1 teaspoon chilli flakes
½ teaspoon cayenne pepper
½ teaspoon salt
½ teaspoon pepper
1 kg skirt steak (cut into large strips)
water
1 bay leaf

Combine dry ingredients and rub into skirt steak. Allow the steak to marinate for 2 hours. Place the steak in a large pot and pour in enough water to just cover the steak. Add a bay leaf and bring to the boil. Once it starts to boil, reduce the heat to low and simmer the steak for 3 hours, or until it easily pulls apart with a fork. Drain the liquid and serve on tacos, huevos rancheros or in quesadillas (or pan-fry for carnitas-style meat).

TACOS
TACO
TACO
Tortillas
Tortillas
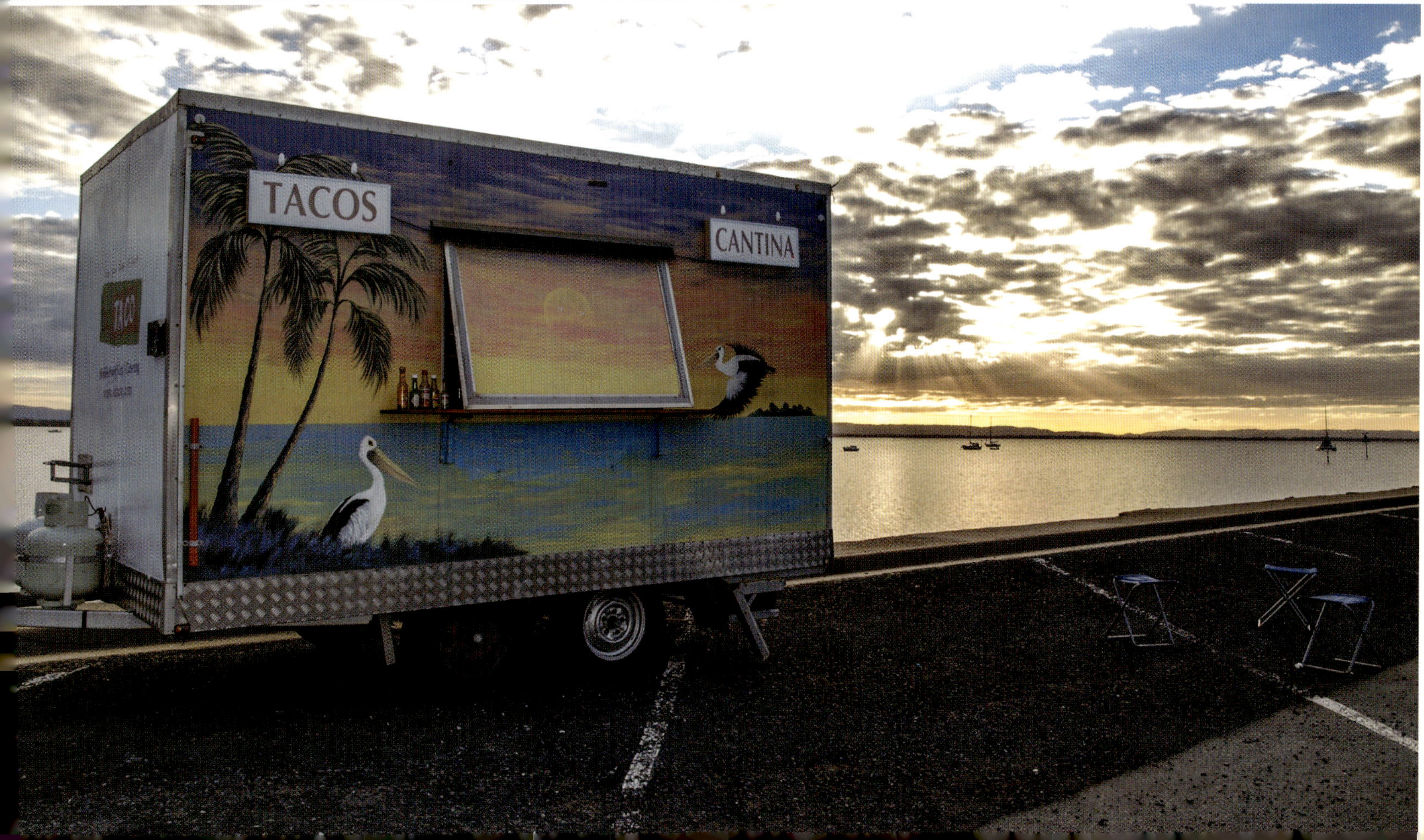
TACOS
CANTINA
TACO

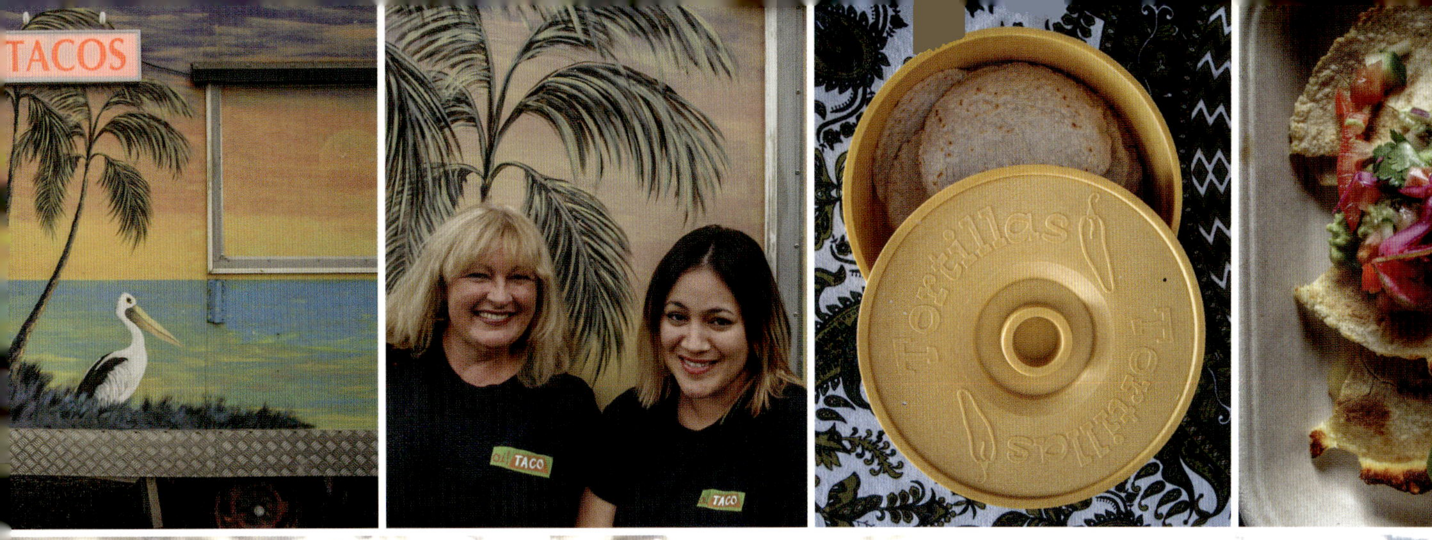

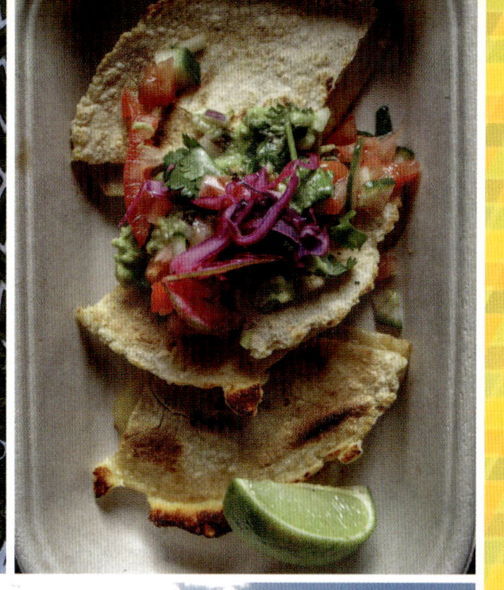

SEÑOR CHURRO

CHIMICHURRI

MAKES 2 CUPS

120 g (2 cups) fresh parsley, finely chopped
7 g (¼ cup) fresh oregano, finely chopped
3 garlic cloves, finely diced
80 ml (⅓ cup) apple cider vinegar
250 ml (1 cup) olive oil
1 tablespoon dried chilli flakes
½ teaspoon ground cumin
1 teaspoon salt

Add all ingredients to a medium-size bowl and stir well.

Note: All herbs must be chopped by hand. Using a food processor bruises the herbs and this gives the chimichurri a different taste.

Argentinean siblings Fernando and Paula came to Australia with their family when they were children. Paula later worked as an accountant for several years, before building up a niche market catering in raw food cakes. Her older brother Fernando was a maintenance operator in the health industry, but in order to maintain a strong link to their heritage through its cuisine, the siblings decided to dedicate their time to bringing Argentinean staples to the streets of Melbourne with Señor Churro.

And while it may have been Paula's husband, Vince, who came up with the idea to start a food truck, the siblings have practised and finessed recipes from their home country to bring locals the classic – and the not-so classic, Aussie-inspired – choripánes (baguettes with chorizo sausage) and churros (long, thin sweet doughnuts). After all, Fernando is not called the churro king without valid reason!

Getting the outer layer of a churro perfectly crunchy, and not oily, while leaving the inside soft and chewy is quite an art. These babies are then dusted with icing sugar, and if you wish, filled with a dulce de leche caramel that the siblings also make themselves. Occasionally, Fernando's wife, Mariel, makes them a batch of alfajores to sell. These time-consuming, delicate treats are made of two crumbly biscuits that are sandwiched together with a dulce de leche filling and then rolled in a chocolate sauce. They are so good, that in all fairness, Mariel must be named the alfajores queen.

LP GAS
STORAGE

SEÑOR CHURRO
ARGENTINIAN street food
CHURROS y CHORIZOS

traditional CHORIZOS
HANDMADE
ARTISANAL
FOOD
authentic
CHORIPAN
GOURMET
CHURROS

TACO CAT

MEXICAN WEDDING COOKIES

MAKES 24

250 g (1 cup) unsalted butter, at room temperature and diced
250 g (2 cups) icing sugar
2 teaspoons pure vanilla extract
300 g (2 cups) plain (all-purpose) flour
1 teaspoon ground cinnamon
½ teaspoon ground cardamom
½ teaspoon ground cloves
½ teaspoon salt
100 g (1 cup) ground almonds

2 tablespoons icing sugar, ¼ teaspoon ground cinnamon
for dusting

Preheat a fan-forced oven to 175°C (190°C conventional/
Gas 5–6). Grease two baking trays (or line with baking paper).

In a large bowl cream the butter and icing sugar until smooth.
Beat in vanilla. Gradually add the flour, cinnamon, cardamom,
cloves and salt. Mix to form a dough. Add the ground almonds
and knead until well mixed. Divide the dough into two. Form
each portion into 2.5 cm wide logs (about the diameter of a
beer bottle!), wrap tightly with plastic wrap and chill in the
refrigerator for approximately 30 minutes, until firm.

Remove the dough logs from the refrigerator. Using a
thin-bladed knife cut each log into 12 equal slices. Place on
baking trays, keeping a 2 cm gap between cookies. Bake for
12–15 minutes or until just beginning to brown. (Check at
10 minutes! These cookies don't take long to cook.) Remove the
cookies from the oven and place on a cooling rack. Leave until
cool enough to handle, but still warm.

Mix extra icing sugar and cinnamon in a small bowl. Using a
small sieve, dust the tops of the cookies with the cinnamon
sugar mixture.

Cookies will keep in an airtight container for 3–5 days.

*Taco Cat owners Benji and Erin
certainly didn't start off in careers
linked to the food industry. Benji
used to be a spray painter, while his
wife Erin still works as a primary
teacher part time. But after living
in Vancouver, Canada for a year
and falling in love with the Mexican
cuisine on offer, they decided to open
their own food truck once back in
Adelaide, Australia.*

*Although they don't have formal
training, Benji and Erin spent time
practising and testing out their
recipes at local markets. They now
proudly make all of the fillings
for their Mexican tacos, including
guacamole, green tomatillo and
pico de gallo salsas, and various hot
sauces using home-grown chillies.*

*With quirky cat-inspired names,
the menu offers 'ChuckLes' – slow-
cooked, shredded beef rib tacos;
the vegetarian/vegan option 'Señor
Gary' – Benji's refried beans, roasted
chunks of potato coated in an Ancho
Chile garlic rub; and 'Sharkos' – fish
tacos using freshly caught shark.*

ADELAIDE MILLING COMPANY
AVIATION
DANGER
KEEP OUT
TACOCAT
0435 451 186

TACOCAT

TREAT YO SELF

AUTHENTIC SALSA VERDE

In Mexico salsa verde means a green sauce made from tomatillos, a fruit that when stripped of its papery husk looks like a green tomato. Sandy loves tomatillos for their sourness! When you combine this with hot green chillies, it becomes the foundation of salsa verde.

Fresh tomatillos are sometimes difficult to find. Most people buy them in tins. If this is the case then roasting them doesn't have the same effect, so boiling them is fine.

SERVES 1–2

5 tomatillos*
1 onion, finely chopped
½ cup fresh coriander, finely chopped
8–10 jalapeños or serrano chillies
1 tablespoon garlic paste

Preheat a fan-forced oven to 180°C (200°C conventional, Gas 6). If you have fresh tomatillos remove the husk and stems; leave the seeds. Slice the tomatillos in half horizontally. Put them in an oven tray and drizzle with oil. Bake them for about 10 minutes, then flip them and bake for another 5 minutes, until the skin starts blistering.

Place all ingredients (including the tomatillos) into a medium-size pot and cover with water. Bring to the boil. Remove from the heat and allow to cool slightly. Transfer the mixture to a blender and blend until smooth. Pour mixture into a clean, airtight container and add salt to taste. The salsa verde can be stored for up to 2 weeks.

** Tomatillos are available from specialty food stores.*

Treat Yo Self owner/operator Sandy was an Australian sailor before starting up her quesadilla and coffee food truck business. Having grown up in a small country town in northern Queensland, she decided at age 18 to join the Royal Australian Navy.

It was while based on the HMAS Manoora that Sandy was affected by two major events that changed the course of her life. The first was helping to bring on board hundreds of refugees during the Tampa affair, the most politically charged refugee case in Australia's recent history. And in the midst of this crisis, the twin towers came down in New York on September 11. Sandy decided she needed a new way to connect with the world, and settled on starting up a food truck business in Melbourne, Australia.

Thanks to an online crowd-funding campaign, Sandy raised enough funds to redesign the exterior of her cart, which was originally a solar juice bar. As such, she inherited an eco-friendly vehicle with solar panels to power up her quesadilla toasters, while the fridge and lights run on generators using vegetable oil for fuel.

Treat Yo Self hit Melbourne's streets in early 2014, and while the menu may be reasonably small, it covers both sweet and savoury quesadillas filled with the like of frijoles negros (black beans) or frijoles refritos (refried beans). Sandy also has a coffee machine in tow to service the local dog-walkers and park-goers.

FLAVOUR FIESTA: *with South American & Mexican amigos*

INDEX

AUTHOR ACKNOWLEDGEMENTS

It's hard to imagine that it was just a little more than a year ago, that I sent Melissa Kayser, a friend and colleague (and now my publisher!), an email one morning, casually suggesting an idea for a book. Little did I realise that this seed of an idea would eventuate into a book that I not only designed and photographed, but researched and wrote all on my own. For this faith and trust I owe Melissa Kayser, Astrid Browne and the team at Hardie Grant Explore much, much gratitude and respect. Thank you for having seen the potential in me to actually pull off such a monumental project.

Thank you, Melissa Kayser, for encouraging me to swim in foreign waters, so to say. Your constant enthusiasm for this project and calm rationality was reassuring, especially during the times that I thought I'd bitten off more than I could chew.

Thank you, Alison Proietto, for your patience and lovely words of encouragement, as well as sorting through and sculpting the mountain of eclectic recipes into a consistent and concise body of text.

Having worked with Megan Ellis, a fellow freelancer, for a number of years I felt completely at ease when she came on board so late in the game, knowing she would tackle the nitty-gritty layout issues, leaving me free to focus on other parts of the book's production.

Thank you to my husband Bernd, who may not quite share my effusive passion for food, but has been endlessly supportive and encouraging, giving me the time and freedom to actively pursue this adventure.

Thank you to my beautiful monkey Maya, who, having had no choice but to accompany me on many research jaunts, has herself become a veritable food critic and fan of food trucks.

I don't quite know where to begin to thank my family and countless friends who have helped me during this project. Your boundless encouragement and unconditional support shown to me in so many ways during this project was truly phenomenal. From looking after our daughter when neither my husband nor I could, feeding us countless delicious home-cooked meals when we were too stressed to even write a shopping list, or the numerous occasions you joined me during my truck chase, either on the road, at truck jams or festivals – it made it all the more fun to have your company. So with too many of you to list, I do hope you all know who you are. I love you dearly and feel incredibly lucky and ever grateful to have such a generous group of family and friends in my life.

I do, however, owe a particular thank you to my beautiful friend Vera Moreira, who not only accompanied me on countless occasions to meet and photograph food trucks but she also gave her time freely and selflessly, helping me in many ways, especially during the last crazy few months when I also had to organise moving to another country for 6 months!

Finally, a big thank you to all the food truck owners. Without your time and willingness to share your stories and recipes with me, there would, of course, be no book. It was truly a pleasure to have gotten to know you. Your generous food offerings were also very appreciated.

Viva la food truck revolution!

ACKNOWLEDGEMENTS

The publisher would like to acknowledge the following individuals and organisations:

Editorial manager
Melissa Kayser

Project manager and editor
Alison Proietto

Editorial assistance
Richard Overall

Layout
Megan Ellis

Pre-press
Megan Ellis, Splitting Image

Photography credits
All images © Erika Budiman except for the following *(left to right, top to bottom, where more than one image appears on a page):*

Pages 15 (b) and (e) Angus Kiley; 27 (d) courtesy Smokin' Barrys; 28 (b) and (d) courtesy Smokin' Barrys; 29 (a) and (b) courtesy Smokin' Barrys; 43 (a)–(d) courtesy the Bun Mobile; 53 (a)–(d) Anthony Tran; 75 (a) Ben Dearnley; 76 (a) Peter Collie; 77 (a) and (b) Ben Dearnley, (c) Peter Collie; 81 (d) Joseph Chow; 93 (c), (f) and (g) courtesy Jafe Jaffles; 95 (h) courtesy the Little Cake Tin; 97 (e) Greg Cartwright; 99 (b) Ellen Rose; 100 (a), (c) and (e) Ellen Rose; 101 (b) Ellen Rose; 103 (h) courtesy Veggie Patch Van; 119 (h) courtesy Greek Street Food; 121 (a) Damien Pleming; 123 (a) Kate Berry, (c) Sonia Lear; 145 (a)–(e) courtesy Comida do Sul; 153 (a)–(e) courtesy Chingón; 154 Vellum Studios; 155 (a)–(d) Vellum Studios; 159 (b) courtesy La Chiva; 160 Chantal Fraser; 161 (a)–(e) Chantal Fraser; 167 (a)–(g) courtesy Taco Cat.

Explore Australia Publishing Pty Ltd
Ground Floor, Building 1, 658 Church Street,
Richmond, VIC 3121

Explore Australia Publishing Pty Ltd is a division of Hardie Grant Publishing Pty Ltd

Published by Explore Australia Publishing Pty Ltd, 2014

Concept, design and text © Erika Budiman, 2014

A Cataloguing-in-Publication entry is available from the catalogue of the National Library of Australia at www.nla.gov.au

ISBN-13 9781741174588

10 9 8 7 6 5 4 3 2 1

Printed and bound in China by 1010 Printing International Ltd

Disclaimer: This book uses metric cup measurements, i.e. 250 ml for 1 cup; in the US a cup is 8 fl oz, just smaller, and American cooks should be generous in their cup measurements; in the UK a cup is 10 fl oz and British cooks should be scant with their cup measurements.

Publisher's note: Every effort has been made to ensure that the information in this book is accurate at the time of going to press. The publisher welcomes information and suggestions for correction or improvement. Email: info@exploreaustralia.net.au

www.exploreaustralia.net.au
Follow us on Twitter: @ExploreAus
Find us on Facebook: www.facebook.com/exploreaustralia